LITTLE THINGS THAT MATTER

LITTLE STEPS TAKEN CONSISTENTLY
CAN MAKE YOUR DREAM COME TRUE

Jerome O. Obode

Unless otherwise indicated, Scripture quotations are taken from the Holy Bible, King James' (Authorized Version). First published in 1611.

Printed in Great Britain in 2018 by Living Spread Publications

Copyright © Jerome O. Obode 2018

All rights reserved. No part of this publication may be reproduced, stored in a retrieval system, or transmitted in any form or by any means without written permission from the publisher.

ISBN 978-1-9998798-1-5

London, United Kingdom

www.livingspread.com

Email: livingspread@gmail.com

Dedication

This book is dedicated to everyone who has struggled to succeed in a big way, who needs to understand that little actions compounded overtime, can dramatically transform their life.

CONTENTS

CHAPTER ONE
   Little Things That Matter   1
CHAPTER TWO
   Little Creatures That Achieve Great Things   12
CHAPTER THREE
   Little Children Who Accomplished Great Things   27
CHAPTER FOUR
   Little Habits That Really Matter   34
CHAPTER FIVE
   Little Foxes Can Ruin A Vineyard   47
CHAPTER SIX
   The Power of the First Step   71
CHAPTER SEVEN
   The Power of Compounded Activities   88
CHAPTER EIGHT
   Keep Making Progress   105
CHPAPTER NINE
   The Power of Little Ideas   112
CONCLUSION   121

NOTES

ACKNOWLEDGEMENTS

Special thanks to the Almighty God for giving me life and the inspiration to write day after day. Thank you, Jesus, for your breath of life.

I am immensely grateful to my dear wife and friend Bola Obode- for your unwavering support, no matter the weather.

Thanks to my children Prince, Bernadette, Samuel and Zoe for being wonderful and loving children. It has been a great joy to be your father.

I am eternally grateful once again to all members of Global Impact Tabernacle, my family Church where I have preached and learned over the years.

God has blessed me tremendously with great friends and partners in ministry. Dr Patrick Odigie and Pastor Mabel Odigie- the impact of your friendship and support to me cannot be measured.

Very special thanks to Drs Ezekiel and Funmi Alawale- you have been friends indeed! I cannot thank you enough.

My other special friends and supporters are too many to mention in a book. Bishop Barth Orji, Bishop Charles Awowoyin; Dr Tony and Pastor Modupe Obayori, Pastors Matthias Basil, Dapo Ayetigbo, Gabriel Diya, Vincent Omusi, Nathaniel Saingbe, Denis Ekagha and Shola Mene- you are all God-given friends. You are highly appreciated.

My heart-felt gratitude to Dapo Ogunwusi, and Paul Pius for your editorial work on the manuscript. Thanks a lot.

FOREWORD

Every morning, like clockwork, I receive short devotional writings from Pastor Jerome. The aptness and brevity of each devotional writing is something that I have come to appreciate and enjoy.

Pastor Jerome is a man of prayer, who understands and moves in the power of God. Many who understand and move in God's power as he does do not naturally give attention to the wisdom of God. I was pleasantly surprised by the depth of God's wisdom packed into each chapter of this book.

Our God is a God of power, and a God of wisdom. The Bible is full of displays of God's amazing and unlimited power by which he transformed and brought changes into impossible situations. What is not obvious to many is that God operated more in wisdom in the Bible than with his power.

With great wisdom, God aggregates and weaves the free actions of men – wicked and good – together into beautiful and wonderful works that bring success and propels his purpose. It is this attribute and ability that is referenced and described in *1 Corinthians 2:8: "But the rulers of this world have not understood it (wisdom of God); if they had, they would not have crucified our glorious Lord. (NLT).*

So, as I read the book, when I came across phrases such as "success is a journey" and a result of aggregation of little efforts, I knew that I was interacting with the wisdom of God.

In reading this book, with my knowledge of Pastor Jerome, I was reminded of the scripture in 1 Corinthians 2:1-6: *"When I first came to you, dear brothers and sisters,[a] I didn't use lofty words and impressive wisdom to tell you God's secret plan.[b] 2 For I decided that while I was with you I would forget everything except Jesus Christ, the one who was crucified. 3 I came to you in weakness— timid and trembling. 4 And my message and my preaching were very plain. Rather than using clever and persuasive speeches, I relied only on the power of the Holy Spirit. 5 I did this so you would trust not in human wisdom but in the power of God. 6 Yet **when I am among mature believers, I do speak with words of wisdom,** but not the kind of wisdom that belongs to this world or to the rulers of this world, who are soon forgotten."*

God has not asked any believer to choose between his power and his wisdom. He has given us this book, which contains things that are normally spoken amongst the mature, to bring us into maturity and lift people out of situations that have affected them for years.

In writing this foreword, I wanted to recommend specific chapters but found myself unable to, because each chapter is loaded with wisdom and faith building principles.

If you are someone who has been waiting for a long time for God's power to miraculously lift you out of your situation, you should read this book.

I was fascinated to read about 'Kaizen' in the book. It is a principle that I have applied in transforming teams and organisations.

If you know anyone who is focused or addicted to instant success, you should recommend or buy a copy of this book for the person.

I have been fascinated by businesses that have endured and lasted for hundreds of years. I was interested in knowing how they have successfully weathered through several seasons of change. If you are aiming to build an enduring business that can weather changes of seasons, there are principles in this book for you.

My last recommendation is for those with children that are in and above their teenage years. You should read this book together as a family so that you can learn and implement the principles together. It will greatly help your family.

God bless!!

Dr Tony Obayori,

Grace Assembly

London, United Kingdom

INTRODUCTION

The Bible says, "...*God has chosen the foolish things of the world to confound the wise; and God hath chosen the weak things of the world to confound the things which are mighty; and base things of the world, and things which are despised, hath God chosen, yea, and things which are not, to bring to nought things* that are: *That no flesh should glory in His presence"* (1 Corinthians 1:27-29). God deliberately chooses to use foolish, weak, base and despised things. He uses even things that do not exist to bring things into existence. God has designed life to be simple, but people tend to make things complicated for themselves. Small wins, little actions and basic steps can add up to bring about awesome and dramatic changes in the lives of people.

One of the reasons many people accomplish little or nothing in life is that they are waiting for that moment when they can take giant strides, bite off big chunks or have plenty of money that will enable them pursue their life goals. Some people feel too little or worthless in their own eyes that they would not even take a step, especially when they see how far others have gone ahead of them. Every great thing starts little. A person who is too afraid to start little has little chance of progressing beyond their current state.

To succeed in life a person needs to be able to value the power of small improvements. Overnight success only happens in people's imagination; what you need are tiny steps in the right direction. We all appreciate babies when they begin to make rarely noticeable progress- like babbling, growing their first tooth, saying mum or dad, or learning to scribble with the pen or pencil for the first time. When babies take their initial one or two steps, we applaud them because we understand that it is the beginning of a new era in child's life that could turn them into the fastest runner in the world. Of course, from little actions we expect babies to grow into doing greater things. In the same way we must learn to appreciate the initial and ongoing steps in our lives that will ultimately lead us into fulfilling our God-given destiny.

Every mountain is climbed one step at a time; every journey begins with the first small step. The tallest buildings in the world started off with a foundation that no one (except the builders) will ever set their eyes upon. Some took months, and others, years to accomplish, but they are the products of daily tiny actions. Whatever you do- whether it is starting a business, buying a home, raising a child, studying for a degree, saving for retirement, it takes daily tiny steps. Every great thing started small, and people who do not understand the power of small beginnings, and continuous daily improvement will never know what it means to succeed. Never feel daunted by the magnitude of what is ahead of you. Start with what you have and where you are today, and you will soon be where you want to be tomorrow.

Dream big, but start small. Have great plans, but have simple steps for accomplishing your plans. Take the first, second, third and fourth steps; keep making progress even in the simplest form and you will be moving towards achieving any dream you may have. No single giant step will bring your dream to pass; it is a succession of small movements that will get you there.

You will come across stumbling blocks in the process, but you must turn them into stepping stones by all means. Sometimes you may find that your tiny steps seem to be leading nowhere, and you may have to start all over; at such times never give up; start all over if need be, and your effort will finally pay off.

Success is a journey, and does not happen by impulse, but by a succession of planned steps. Success is the total of little efforts accumulated over a period of time. If you do not get started you will never get ahead; one tiny step today may not get you to your destination immediately, taking them daily will get you there before you realise it.

I was inspired to write this book when I fully understood and experienced that a successful and happy life is the outcome of daily little actions. I became burdened to put my thoughts and experience into a book when I observed that a great number of people that I know are simply waiting for something big to happen in their lives. Simplify your day, week, month and year into simple and achievable daily actions. Make it so easy you cannot fail to achieve them. Be so persistent about carrying out the actions you will never miss more than one day a time. Get so focused about your daily schedule that nothing in the world is important enough to derail your plan. Make that move and things will start to move in the direction you desire.

CHAPTER ONE

LITTLE THINGS THAT MATTER

You have probably heard it said before, 'pay attention to details', or 'the devil is in the details. In many things we do in life the battle is usually with the details. Little and often neglected things tend to hold sway over many other factors of success. The pennies, the minutes and the minutest elements of every major endeavour actually hold the key to our success. If you are not thorough with little things, you are unlikely to be victorious in bigger ones. When people fail to pay attention to little things, it is usually the beginning of failure in doing greater things. Every great thing and every great person started small. No one ever starts from the top. Many things in life are designed to develop progressively. People who ignore simple things are more likely to face challenges when attempting noble tasks.

Life is made up of seconds, minutes, days, weeks, months and years. You cannot effectively use your minutes unless you take hold of the seconds. It is impossible to successfully utilise your hours unless you can manage your minutes. Many days, weeks, months and years will slip off your grip if you fail to have a firm grasp of your hours.

Life starts from the common to the uncommon, the known to the unknown, the ordinary to the extraordinary and from the peripheral to the principal. No tree ever grows tall in one day, no matter how fast it grows. No skyscrapers were ever erected in one day. Some took several years to complete. A space craft takes years to manufacture. No truly great thing is achieved in a twinkle. Great achievements stem from small activities. The project you want to take on today will require patient, persistent and progressive action. All mega achievements derive from meagre commitments. People do not grow their confidence or expertise overnight- they start small, grow more and become more. Many people struggle to achieve their dreams because they have been waiting for that 'lucky' day, when they will make a big leap into their breakthrough. Consequently, they fail to take advantage of several opportunities that come their way which could have changed their lives.

It would be absurd for anyone to suggest that big things are not important, or must not be pursued. Greatness and doing great things lie within every one of us, but for many, the thought of setting out to work our way from obscurity to popularity is a daunting and uphill task. The fear of doing what is required to accomplish enormous things can be intimidating and paralysing. The feeling that there is a 'giant' ahead to be conquered frightens the daylight out of the vast majority of God's people. We easily forget the account of David (a young person) who killed the dreaded Goliath, the enemy of God and Israel, with a very little, insignificant weapon- a sling and a stone.

> *David prevailed over the Philistine with a sling and with a stone, and smote the Philistine, and slew him; but there was no sword in the hand of David."* (1 Samuel 17:50).

Just because there is no sword in your hand, does not mean you cannot kill a Goliath. You can do great things from your current position. You can steadily achieve your grand dreams by mastering the elementary stages. Failure is not always because the challenges are too complex, but because people fail to find simple ways to progressively pursue their life dreams. This is the root cause of failure in life.

God wants you to go after your 'Goliath', the enemy of your dream, the challenge ahead of you, the battle you are facing in life, the problem that has weighed you down for years- by the power of the Holy Spirit.

Fortunately, when you walk with God, you do not need a gigantic sword to kill a giant. Little, strategic, smart and persistent steps are all you need to get to your destination.

Every one cowered when Goliath, the Philistine challenged the people of Israel to send a representative who would engage him in a fight. If Goliath defeated the Israelite, Israel would lose the battle. Conversely if the Israelite soldier defeated Goliath, then the Philistines would lose the battle. No one showed up from Israel, until little David with only a sling and stones dared the giant. Get ready to win in every area of life. Be prepared to take the first step no matter how little it is. Little things do really matter. God's blessings coming upon your unrecognisable, basic actions can make all the difference to your success, so long as you take the steps in the right direction.

God Used Little Things in the Bible

All through the Bible we see God demonstrate His ability and willingness to use seemingly unimportant things as the source of great blessings. In Exodus, we see God preparing Moses for a very substantial work. His assignment was to deliver the people of Israel from Egyptian bondage, and lead them into the Promised Land. Apart from God overlooking and overriding Moses' weakness, He also demonstrated His power through something that was lacking in importance - a mere rod.

> *And the LORD said unto him, what is that in thine hand? And he said, A rod."* (Exodus 4:2)

With that rod Moses performed incredible miracles. He produced snakes by simply throwing down the rod. He turned all of the water in Egypt into blood and filled them with frogs by holding out the rod over them. There are many other instances in the Bible where God proved seemingly unimportant or worthless objects can turn out to be powerful instruments in His hands, showing that your little steps or acts can be used by Him to bring you into greatness if you put your trust in Him.

1. Samson slew a thousand Philistines with the jaw bone of an ass (Judges 15:15)
2. The widow of Zarephath fed Elijah and her family with just a handful of flour and a little oil (1Kings 17:17)
3. A cloud the size of a man's hand led to a downpour after Elisha prayed for rain following a two-and-a-half-year draught in Israel (1Kings 18:44)
4. Jesus fed thousands of people with only five loaves and two small fish (John 6:9)
5. God says we must not despise the days of small things (Zechariah 4:10)

6. 'Mustard seed' faith can be used by God to bring about enormous blessings (Matthew 13:32)
7. God uses base and irrelevant things so that no one can share the glory with Him (1Corinthians1: 27)

God will turn your weakness into strength and use your tiny efforts to help you reach your goal. He will meet you where you are, and make something noteworthy out of your life. What small steps are you prepared to take today? What is that mountain before you? How long is the journey you have been struggling to undertake, and how big is the project you have been too afraid to embark upon? Just take the first step, the next, and then things will begin to gather momentum and work in your favour. Do not aim to do too much at a time. You must never despair or be discouraged simply because you have an overwhelming task ahead of you, whether it is something to give up or something to build up. There is always room for improvement. Start small and continue to grow until you reach your goal. The key is to begin, continue, persist and complete. You are never too old to start from the beginning, you are never too young to embark on success journey; it is never too late to start from somewhere. A Chinese proverb says,

"It is better to take small steps in the right direction than to make a great leap forward only to stumble backward."

We all started as a tiny speck in our mothers' womb and grew to become the great and accomplished adults that many of us are today. Starting little or taking little steps does not equate mediocrity. It is simple and steady actions that culminate in significant accomplishments. Many seemingly insignificant steps have made impressive impact on the world and the way we live. Little acts continued and compounded over an extended period is what you need to build your desired future.

When a child is born, it takes weeks and months to get to the point where the child begins to walk, starting with the first few steps. Then parents will begin to look forward to other areas such as commencing school. The child goes to kindergarten, continues through elementary and eventually completes higher education- a very long process requiring a lot of patience. It all involves little steps until the final stage is reached. At each level of education teachers design and implement tiny plans within an overall scheme. These tiny steps- initial assessment, individual learning plans, ongoing and final assessments all make up the package of the entire plan. These elements mingle to determine the final outcome of a student's learning process.

Skipping or ignoring any stage of the master plan can destabilise the process and distort the final outcome. Every one of us has been created to do outstanding things, but none of us has the ability to become distinguished in any field in the twinkling of an eye. It is alright to want to accomplish massive things, but you should be prepared to start small, by taking the first step. These steps may not be significant. They may also not be noticeable at the early stage. Keeping up with them however, and continuing to move in the right direction will, over time lead to big achievements. The answer to walking to the top of any stairs is to take one step after the other no matter how steep or high the flight of stairs. If you overburden yourself at the initial phase of anything, worrying about the amount of energy, time and resources it will take to accomplish your goal, you will find many reasons why your dream is unachievable.

The British Olympic Cycling team: The Power of Little Changes

The British Olympic cycling team did incredibly well when they took everyone by surprise during the Summer Olympics of 2012 in London. The team's performance director, Dave Brailsford attributed their astonishing success to what he referred to as the "aggregation of marginal gains." A 1 percent margin for improvement in everything you do. He believed that if his team made a 1 percent improvement in every area that related to cycling, the total of the small gains would lead to remarkable improvement and laudable achievements in their bid for medals.

It was Brailsford's belief that by making these small consistent improvements, the British cycling team would be able to win the tour de France in 5 years, but he got it wrong! The team won the tour the France in 3 years. Not only did they spring that surprise, in the same year (2012) the British Cycling team dominated the cycling event at the Olympic Games by winning 70 percent of the total gold medals available for the sport. The question is how did they do it? They began by improving on the nutrition of riders and on the training programmes. They also enhanced certain aspects of the bike such as the seat and the weight of the tires. They went on to shape up often ignored areas such as the type of pillow that would give the most comfort when they sleep, and finding out the most suitable type of massage gel.

The search for the 1 percent improvement even covered such aspects as the most effective way to wash hands and minimise the risk of infection. The riders took these 1 percent improvements seriously. In the end just a little change in every aspect brought them to the limelight. It shows that little things can yield big results. If carried through, slight adjustments can lead to huge success. This approach underscores the importance of making continuous improvement by carrying out simple, imperceptible adjustments to the way we live or pursue our goals.

It is easy to forget that everything about life, desirable or undesirable, originates from the small decisions a person makes or continues to make. People generally embrace the idea that unless they are able to bite off big chunks, take long strides or make long jumps, they are not likely to turn their lives around. Whether you want to be financially free, lose weight, study for a degree or simply become a person of influence in any area, you must embrace the saying that 'Rome was not built in a day'.

The British cycling example shows that meticulously applied, a 1 percent adjustment steadily carried out will make you a winner whatever you do. Be encouraged to look for that area of your life where you need that improvement. The Bible says,

> *"For who hath despised the day of small things? For they shall rejoice, and shall see the plummet in the hand of Zerubbabel..."* *(Zechariah 4:10)*.

Never accept that it is too late, even if this is the case in some aspect of your life. You should be able to find a point where you can enforce the 1 percent that will re-shape your life. This concept can also work in the reverse. A 1 percent consistent decline engineered by bad habits can eventually lead to failure, with a person's life going in the wrong direction. Let us look a little closely at the above Scripture. Zerubbabel was one of the few leaders God raised to lead the Israelites in returning from Babylonian captivity. They had responsibility to rebuild the temple which was destroyed and abandoned for many years. Zechariah was God's chosen prophet tasked to encourage Zerubbabel in the project. It was a fearful, difficult task to carry out. God therefore encouraged Zerubbabel in Zechariah 4:6, *"Not by might nor by power, but by My Spirit,' says the LORD of hosts."* This great task was like a mountain before Zerubbabel, and the Lord promised that the great mountain would be made plain (verse 7) before Zerubbabel. God promised through Prophet Zechariah that just as:

> *"The hands of Zerubbabel have laid the foundation of this great house; his hands shall also finish it ..."*

God knew that humanly speaking, rebuilding the temple at the time was not an easy job. However, all that God wanted was for Zerubbabel to take the first step by starting from somewhere and never giving up. God's power would come upon his efforts and the mountain would turn to a plain and the job at hand completed. God has a purpose for your life. Your dreams are important to Him and He would stand with you whatever you step out to do. If you have a dream, go for it; if you have a desire, take the first steps towards achieving it because God who has begun a good work in you will complete it.

CHAPTER TWO

LITTLE CREATURES THAT ACHIEVE GREAT THINGS

Small does not equate less value, failure or weakness. Some of the most powerful and deadliest creatures are very small. Some of the wisest creatures humans can learn from are also very small. This chapter focuses on learning lessons from some of the smallest creatures on earth- the ant, the spider, the Coney and the locust. These tiny creatures have been used by God to teach us valuable lessons about life and success. Whenever you feel irrelevant, inadequate, rejected and disempowered, you always remember that if God can make these little creatures survive, thrive and excel He will also do it for you. Proverbs 30:24-28 is filled with very powerful lessons for every child of God:

> *"There be four things which are little upon the earth, but they are*

> *exceeding wise: The ants are a people not strong, yet they prepare their meat in the summer; The conies are but a feeble folk, yet make they their houses in the rocks; The locusts have no king, yet go they forth all of them by bands; The spider taketh hold with her hands, and is in kings' palaces."*

Let us examine each of these animals a little more. They may not look great but great people can learn from them.

The Ant (Proverbs 30:25)

Proverbs tell us that ants are not strong species, yet they prepare their food or supplies in the summer. This suggests that no one should allow personal limitations to stop them in any way. Personal weaknesses should not rob anyone of their destiny. You may not be able to achieve massive things at the same time and pace as others, but with planning and consistency your little steps can lead to great things. There are many lessons to learn from the ant, but let us look at a few.

They are purposeful

Each ant focuses on one job- to supply food for the entire family. Full stop. They do not allow for distraction. No televisions, no Facebook, no unwanted guests or anything that is not part of the game plan. If you have a dream or an objective and focus on it, it may take some time to achieve, but lessons from ants suggest that slow and steady can still win if we continue in the right direction without distractions. Speed and volume are important but consistency is the key to great feats.

Team Work

Ants are capable of working individually, but they know their strength lie in working together as a united force towards a common goal. So they go for it. They believe in networking, liaising with and learning from others. Anything you set out to do, someone else may be better or more experienced at it. You can call them up, read their books, read their blogs and attend their seminar classes. You may if need be, pay for their services. Get whatever it is that you can get from others to reach your goal.

If you belong to a group, other people will rely on your cooperation and contributions to make progress and accomplish their goals. Small groups can do great things so long as they stay united, consistent, and strive towards the same direction.

Time Management

Ants are good time managers. They hide and rest away from cold, harsh winter, but in the summer they muster all their energies, gather all the food they can using all the time they have for productive purposes. It is important to know and do what we should at the right time and place. This is very critical to success. Occasional chunks of activities will achieve far less than small consistent actions on an ongoing basis.

Ants Think Big But Take Small Steps

Ants are small but are by no means small in their thinking. This book is about doing magnificent things through seemingly insignificant steps; it is about the impact little actions (positive or negative) carried out over a long period can make on our lives. Ants build great colonies. They build gigantic hills, but they do this by moving forward in ways too small to be noticed. Anyone who thinks big, breaks a project into little steps, stay focused and remain progressive will not be easily stopped by anything. Every ordinary person can achieve extraordinary things. Some people think big, however, they feel daunted by the scope and size of the task ahead to the point that they lose heart and never take the first step they need to succeed.

Ants are Strategic and Forward Looking

We can learn strategy and foresight from the ants: *"Go to the ant, thou sluggard; consider her ways, and be wise: Which having no guide, overseer, or ruler, provideth her meat in the summer, and gatherest her food in the harvest"* (Proverbs 6:6-8).

Ants maximise opportunities, think ahead and display great wisdom. They teach us to think ahead and not to be overtaken by events. Having a big goal broken into little doable steps is very crucial to success. Never be afraid to go for the top or the best. As long as you can reduce your dream into tiny daily steps, you will get there. The things we avoid today simply because they are difficult, scary, painful and frustrating will never go away. Running away from them will not help us to truly escape; it is better to tackle challenges and limitations head on, one step at a time, one chunk at a time, a little bit every day.

Ants Never Give Up

Mountains cannot stop the ant. They are not intimidated by the size of any problem, opponent or task. If they run into an obstacle they will try to climb over, climb around or dig under. One way or the other the ant must find a way of escape. Size may be a problem for you, availability of resources may also put you at a disadvantage, but if you can persist like the ant and depend on God to help you find a way out, little, slow, but steady efforts will ultimately pay off. The secret is to keep trying, never give up on yourself, never slow down, never look back, and God will make a way for you. If God can help these small creatures to overcome their weaknesses and obstacles, He will also help you turn your weaknesses into strength.

The Coney (Proverbs 30:26)

The Coney or rock badger is a wise little rodent that lives in the rocky hills. They are weak, frightened and timid; they are naturally incapable of doing great things because they are feeble in make-up and small in size. Yet they are able to survive in dangerous circumstances and are capable of providing for, and protecting themselves. They accept that they are weak, but also accept that they must not let this disadvantage stand in their way towards fulfilment, happiness and achievement. Their feeble nature never weighs them down. They stay safe and protected by using their God-given instincts and wisdom. They escape to the rocks and hide at the slightest hint of danger. There must be something you can do to elevate yourself, an aspect of life where you are good. It may seem insignificant to you, and may not be recognised or appreciated by others. Discover, develop and deploy your strengths and do something worthwhile. Let no giants deter you from entering into your promise land. Let no difficult terrain terrify you. Hide yourself in, and draw from the Rock that never fails, Jesus Christ. You are alright just the way you are, build upon that little thing that you have- develop it and make something out of it. Take the first step, take the next and continue until you hit your target.

Let God turn your weakness into strength. In a world of much stronger, more educated, more privileged and better resourced people, if you give your weaknesses back to God, He will make something beautiful out of it. If you keep worrying about what you do not have, how unprepared you are and how limited your chances are in a very competitive environment, you will be tempted to fold your arms and do nothing. If you continue to think that your product or output will not be as good as others' you may never attempt anything worthwhile. Everyone is special and everyone can do unique things in their own stride and their own way which God can turn into something significant.

The Locust (Proverbs 30:27)

The Locusts teach us a sense of unity. They have no king or leader, yet they move together in groups. They understand that there is strength in unity- whether in Church or any other organisation. There is strength in being united within you- spirit, soul and body. Your Spirit must be whole and sound, and transformed by God's Word if you want God's power to influence your life. Your spirit must constantly remain in tune with God so that you can draw strength and nourishment for your entire being. A sound mind will assure you that God means what He says in His Word concerning you, but a doubting and weak mind will influence you in a negative way. Your mind must dream it, believe it and pursue it. Your body should be ready to bear the physical pain, burden and hard work required to carry everything through. You need to develop the social skills required to connect and relate effectively because without the relevant people, your progress will be limited. Take advantage of the potential input from the people that surround you. You need to work in agreement with God's Word to take you to your next level. Work with the Father, Son and the Holy Spirit. Draw strength from God and from everyone God has placed within your reach. One of the greatest lessons from the locust is the power of a united force. Jesus says where two or three are gathered in His name, He is there in their midst. He says if two people shall unite and ask anything they want, His heavenly Father will move on their behalf.

The Spider (Proverbs 30:28)

The spider is also a vulnerable, humble but ambitious little creature. It is very skilful- hence it can design those complex structures called web. Although the spider has no remarkable pace, even if you destroy its web it will start all over again, design and build a new web. To fully destroy a spider's web you will have to completely eliminate the spider. The web is both its home and hunting tool. Spiders can inhabit and survive in pretty much everywhere- in mountains and valleys, in extreme cold or extreme heat, in trees, cracks and crevices, and in the most unusual places, whether they are welcome or not. Nobody wants spiders in their homes, but this does not deter them from finding their way and crafting their web in your home. Despite the fact that spiders may be weak and feeble, God has built into them everything they need to survive and thrive in hostile and difficult terrains. No matter your shortcomings, there is something in you that God can use to lift you over the barriers you face. Find that thing and work at it.

The Bible even says the spider lives in kings' palaces. It shows that no matter how unwanted, rejected and powerless you may feel, with God you still stand the chance of making it to the top. All you need is a life of purpose, focus and determination. You can still rise high and get to the pinnacle of your dreams and calling. Nothing will stop you.

Never feel too little or too feeble to make a difference to your generation. You have a place to fill. Everybody is unique. Some are unique in great ways, while others are unique in modest ways. Those who feel and act great will do great things. Those who do not quite feel that way can still think big, take little and consistent steps and make history. You need to accept that you cannot be someone else, but being who you are and working on whom you are can take you as far as you desire in life. You do not have to reach the finishing point at the same time with the fastest runners; but start your own race, persist until you finish.

There is something to learn from every one of the above creatures. Little things can be very powerful in doing astounding and remarkable things.

The ant teaches us to think about the future- whether it is about heaven, our profession, children or retirement. The future will always come. The Coney or rock badger is vulnerable but puts its trust in hiding places in the rocks, to which it runs promptly for cover just like we should all trust in, and run into cover in the Rock of Ages and never be afraid of failure. The locust teaches us about unity. Everyone needs to work together and stay connected. More importantly, you should be in complete unity with your spirit, soul and body so you can go as far as you want in life. The spider teaches us to acknowledge but ignore our weaknesses. It points to the ability of God to take us to higher heights if we would depend on Him. Being little does not equate to incapacity. Weaknesses and inadequacies should not preclude you from success, from going after your dream.

The Little Boy and the Star Fish

You may be familiar with the following story, but a story retold refreshes the memory and remind us to do something we need to do.

There was once an old man who had the habit of walking the beach morning after morning before beginning his day's business. As he did his usual walk one morning after a big storm, he saw a massive spread of starfish over a large expanse of the beach, stretching over either direction. Far away, his eyes caught a little boy coming towards him. As the boy approached, he paused intermittently, bending and picking up certain objects and throwing them into the sea. As the boy drew closer, the man greeted, "Good morning! If I may ask, what is it that you are doing?"

Looking up, the boy took a break and answered, "Throwing star fish into the ocean. The tide had washed them up onto the beach and they can't return to the sea by themselves. When the sun gets high, they will die, unless I throw them back into the water."

Then the old man said, "But there must be tens of thousands of starfish on this beach. I'm afraid you won't really be able to make much a difference." Bending low again, the boy lifted another starfish, and one more time, threw it into the ocean.

Returning and smiling to the old man, the little boy said, "It made a difference to that one!" You can change the world by taking those insignificant steps. Even if you do not make everything happen, you can make something happen- one day at a time, one step at a time, one action at a time, one person at a time and towards one cause at a time. Your action will probably make a little difference, but that tiny difference could translate into big victory in someone else's world.

If you have often wondered how much your contribution can make, this story will probably answer your question. If you have been waiting to be able do something dramatic before you act, you should have a rethink. If you have always felt you need all the time, resources and preparation before making a contribution or starting that project, let this story encourage you to start something today. Take your eyes off the size of the task ahead and begin to put in the meagre input you can today. You should be:

"... confident of this one thing, that He which hath begun a good work in you will perform it until the day of Jesus Christ" (Philipians1:6). Do not let size stop you- whether your own size or the size of the problem. You can still do uncommon exploits by doing ordinary things consistently and incrementally. You do not have to be a perfectionist. Many perfectionists hardly give themselves the

opportunity to practice and make improvement. They tend to have an all-or-nothing approach to issues. They end up doing nothing because of the fear of not having a perfect start. The only way to be perfect is to practice and the only way to practice is to act. Your aim must be continuous improvement, progress and meeting your personal targets. Be happy with who you are today and make the most of it. Tomorrow will be better if you put all your energies into doing what you can today and leave the rest to God.

For the Want of a Pin

A typical illustration of the power of little things can be seen in the crash of two BOEING 747 cargo planes in 1991 and 1992. The reason for the crashes were established to be faulty 4-inch-long pins which were used by the aircraft manufacturers for mounting the plane engines.

In 1997 Boeing received reports of cracks in the fuse pins that attach engines to wings. Boeing created stronger pins but some airlines opted for the old pins instead. Then December, 29 1991 China Airlines Boeing 747 freighter using the new pins crashed killing five people. Also on October 4, 1992 EL AL Israel Airlines cargo plane lost two engines and crashed killing 4 crew and 39 people on the ground.

Air Accident investigation later revealed that a design flaw on the 4-inch-long pin that held the engine in place was to blame for these disasters. The pins were meant to keep the engines from falling off the wing of the airplane. The pins were designed to severe in the event of a crash, instead, in these instances they broke when the planes were up in the air. Boeing have some of the greatest and most reliable aircraft in the world, yet the tiny pin incidents could have tarnished their image and raised serious safety alarm. Although they later fixed the problem, the events clearly show that some things that appear not-so-important could sometimes have grave impact on our lives.

What is that little thing that has been having the most impact on your life in a negative way?

What can you do to minimise or eliminate the threat? What is that little thing that could have the most positive impact on your life? In what ways can you maximise the potential benefits that you can get from it? What are the small steps you can take on a regular basis that will ultimately change your life?

"For the want of a nail the shoe was lost,

For the want of a shoe the horse was lost,

For the want of horse, the rider was lost,

For the want of a rider the battle was lost,

For the want of a battle the kingdom was lost,

And all for the want of a horseshoe-nail.

    -Benjamin Franklin

For the want of a nail the kingdom was lost is a proverb related to a battle in which the loss of something as trivial as the horse-shoe nail led to the loss of a battle, and ultimately the loss of a kingdom. Failing to pay attention to minute details can be the undoing of any one, any organisation and any project.

In the same way that seconds result in minutes, hours and days, so also can some things we pay the least attention to, accumulate to dictate what happens eventually in our lives.

CHAPTER THREE

LITTLE CHILDREN WHO ACCOMPLISHED GREAT THINGS

Little things, little actions and little children are not often taken seriously, but as I have been discussing in this book, many things that we ignore can significantly impact our lives for good or bad. Many inventions or discoveries that have changed our lives are so tiny an uninformed person could ignore them.

In this section, I will briefly examine some of the contributions that little children have made to society. When thinking of great achievements, it is easy to write off little children no matter how smart they are. They are often seen as being more dependent on others, and not much is usually expected of them. However, history has proved this is not always the case. Children of varying ages have achieved great things that many adults or older people can only imagine in their life time. Given the right exposure, support and encouragement, children can do awesome things that many adults could only dream of. Many of the limitations faced by a number of children are those imposed upon them by parents, guardians and society who fail to understand that young people's dreams are not always mere fantasies. The Bible states:

> *"Josiah was eight years old when he began to reign, and he reigned in Jerusalem one and thirty years. And he did that which was right in the sight of the LORD, and walked in the ways of David his father, and declined neither to the right hand, nor to the left. For in the eighth year of his reign, while he was yet young, he began to seek after the God of David his father: and in the twelfth year he began to purge Judah and Jerusalem from the high places, and the groves, and the carved images, and the molten images"* (2 Chronicles 34:1-3).

Definitely, the young king would have been under the help of minders and tutors, nevertheless his case is an indication that young people can be guarded and supported to do great things. Jesus never overlooked little children. They had a place in His heart, because as the Maker He knows there is no limit to what God can do through them. When God turns His light on little children, they will work wonders, some will do more remarkable things than many adults. We need to all take responsibility for the children God has put under our care. Adults tend to spend a lot more time on themselves- building their own skills and dreams. Too many times the little ones are hardly given attention and adequate opportunities, partly because we do not want to put too much pressure on them. Some other times it is because we are too busy thinking about ourselves that only left-over time and resources are directed towards them.

God will do Great things through our Children

We see examples all through the Bible, of God doing great things through children. It is not about age, strength or knowledge. God can bless your little efforts. God has no problem using the weak or strong. He will use the timid, frigid or rigid. He will use just about anything and anyone. The Bible says:

> *"Out of the mouths of babes and sucklings hast thou ordained strength because of thine enemies, that thou mightest still the enemy and the avenger"* (Psalm 8:2)

I believe Jesus was also talking about God's ability to use anything and anybody, including little children. You do not have to have a great background to become great in life. You do not have to be perfectly trained and ready before you can be your best in life. Training and preparation are important as long as they are directly related to your goals. Babes and suckling in the above passage symbolise insignificance, irrelevance, and defects. They refer to those who have been written off and people you never thought would go far in life. When God's power touches them, He makes something beautiful out of their lives.

Never write off little children. God can demonstrate His greatness through them. Parents, leaders and everyone who takes responsibility for young people, little children in particular, should search and discover the greatness that God has invested in them; discover, develop and deploy the gifts God has deposited in them. This should be done deliberately, painstakingly and consistently. Here are a few examples of children and young people used by God in the Bible:

- Jesus used the five loaves and two fish of a lad to feed over five thousand people (John 6:9)
- Daniel and his three young friends resolved not to contaminate themselves with the king's food (Daniel chapter 1)
- God called Jeremiah (as a child) into the prophetic ministry (Jeremiah 1:5-7)

- As a boy, David fought and defeated the dreaded Goliath the most powerful fighter among the Philistines (1Samuel 17:33)
- It was the Apostle Paul's young nephew that warned him of a Jewish plot to kill him when he became converted and preached the gospel of Jesus Christ (Acts 23:16-22)

These are only a few of the examples that God can use little ones to make things happen, to demonstrate His power and change the lives of others. When deliberately prepared and guided, the Bible says *"as arrows in the hand of a warrior, so are the children of one's youth."* Psalm 127:4

Samantha Smith: America's Youngest Ambassador

Samantha Smith was born June 1972. When she was 10 years old she was well aware from the news, about the cold war and the tensions between the United States and the Soviet Union. She wrote a letter in1982 to the then Soviet leader, Yuri Andropov, in which she asked to know why Soviet and U.S relations were so tense that they could lead to a nuclear war. She wanted to know what the Soviet leader would do to prevent a nuclear war with America.

Excerpts of her letter were published in the Soviet media, but she never received an answer from the

Soviet leader. She took a step further and wrote to the Soviet Ambassador to the United States, asking to know why his country's leader had not replied to her letter. Following this, the Soviet leader, Yuri Andropov replied to Samantha Smith's letter promising that his country would not attack any country with nuclear weapons unless it was first attacked. Mr Andropov invited Ms Smith to the Soviet Union, an invitation she accepted. Samantha Smith became a peace activist as a child, travelling all over the world with the help of her parents. Unfortunately, she died at a tender age of 13 after a commercial plane in which she and her father were travelling crashed. After her death the Soviet government issued a postage stamp with her picture on it. Every child under our care is a special gift from God and must be nurtured, and encouraged to fulfil God's purpose in their generation. It is not enough to feed, and care for them; we have to do more to channel and direct them to accomplish incredible things for God and humanity.

Thandiwe Chama: The Education Rights Activist

At 8 years old, after her school in Zambia was closed down due to lack of teachers, Thandiwe refused to let go. She mobilised 60 children to scout for another school. The result was that all of the 60 children were given a place in another school. From that point onwards, this young child became an education activist. Not only was she out and about speaking and persuading people and authorities on education, she also spoke on important issues such as AIDS. As a result of her fight to ensure educational and other rights for children, Thandiwe made herself popular all over the world. In 2007 she was awarded the International Children's Peace Prize for her courageous and tireless fight for children's rights even at a tender age of 16.

Give Little Children a Chance

God is very interested in using little children for the cause of the kingdom. All through the Bible we see God's power move through them, we see God use them to accomplish great things for His Kingdom. Little wonder, the devil also takes keen interest in these instruments. We read of stories all over the world of how Satan recruits children for his evil agenda. He utilises children for witchcraft and other spiritual operations. Satan influences little children into committing heinous crimes- including murder, rape, robbery, arson and other types of evil. Satan can use little children for every conceivable crime. This is the more reason why as God's people we must let God work through us to prepare and deploy them (as early as possible) to do great things for God. Little children have a very special place in the heart of God. He wants to demonstrate His power through them.

CHAPTER FOUR

LITTLE HABITS THAT REALLY MATTER

The Oxford English dictionary defines habit as:

"A settled or regular tendency or practice, especially one that is hard to give up." A habit is a recurring pattern of behaviour which may be developed through repetitive action, and can be reinforced by a permanent state of mind. Habits can be either bad or good. Negative habits are damaging and unproductive and often lead to setback, whereas good habits are the ingredients that success is made of. Most habits usually appear harmless and insignificant but they build up over a long time to make us who we are and determine the outcome of our lives.

Negative habits are never harmless. Their impact may not be conspicuous in the short term but in the long term the 'devil' in bad habits will begin to surface- in many cases this will not happen until the habit has taken deep roots into a person's life. Positive habits also follow the same pattern. Initially you may not see the contributions the habit makes to your life but if you stay with it for a long time, the results can be astonishing. Habits are very easy to develop and with the passage of time, their power over a person will become stronger and more difficult to abandon. Any old habit can be thrashed and new ones developed.

Negative habits such as sleeping late, watching too much TV, unnecessary web search, obsession with social network sites, and poor use of time will adversely affect a person's productivity and success. On the other hand, good habits such as healthy eating, learning to appreciate others, and finding a few minutes daily to read a book, will set you up for success.

Why People Embrace Negative Habits

Destructive habits are much easier to develop than productive ones. One of the reasons for this is that unhelpful habits require less effort as opposed to rewarding ones which require discipline and consistency. The fallen human nature has a tendency to gravitate towards negativity. Human beings are naturally resistant to change or anything that invites them to venture into unknown territories. Moreover, the results of negative habits take time to be noticed in people's lives, so it is possible to drift further without knowing it.

Another reason people fail to change old habits is because they personally desire certain things and ways of life, which they are not prepared to give up. Hence, they pretend the situation is alright and change is not needful. Unless a person is aware of and has accepted the need to change, and is prepared to change, they will not be able to embark on the journey of habit replacement. Eventually, what began as tiny, insignificant and inconsequential behaviours, will soon wrap around an individual till they wreak havoc in the person's life, and the chains become too strong to break.

Little and Consistent Habits

Whatever your dream or goal, small or great you will need to form positive habits that will gradually lead you there. One of the reasons behind many failure and countless unfulfilled dreams is that people feel overwhelmed by the enormity of their dream or the magnitude of a problem. You can change anything; you can do anything; anything that anyone can achieve is absolutely within your grasp. You only need to drop the idea that you must do it in a big way to achieve big time. Not necessarily so, mini habits consistently developed over a period of time lead to continuous minor victories. Most major victories you see out there are the combined effect of smaller ones that have gone unnoticed. Micro victories accumulated or compounded over time will result in massive gains and grand achievements. If you disregard little accomplishments you will risk your chance of becoming great because little things always play a major part in our success.

You can find easier and less challenging ways to climb that mountain no matter how long it takes. It takes one step at time and developing simple and relevant habits. So long as you are making progress, sooner or later you will hit your mark. There is nothing wrong with aiming high, but aiming too high than you are ready for can very quickly dissipate your energy and complicate matters for you. Your esteem and morale can be badly damaged if you take on too much and fail too soon. Set baby goals and grow into it by developing that habit needed to see things through.

Start from Somewhere

If you fail to start from somewhere you will eventually get nowhere. Make a list of your most important tasks, three or at most five is recommended. Make a plan to do something about each one in a small way every day, and preferably at designated times. If you have been having problems entering into a regime of exercise to help you stay fit and lose weight, why not take a walk round your neighbourhood for just five minutes a day in the first instance. Do this for a number of days until you become comfortable. You can then take it further by adding a few more minutes or extending the distance covered, until you feel ready and inclined to take on more challenge. What many smart and highly motivated people can do within a short period, anyone else can do by breaking it down into tiny and continuous steps.

If you have been using too much sugar, maybe two, three or even four teaspoons at a time, why not cut it by half a teaspoon for at least twenty-one days before taking on the challenge of cutting out one tea spoon and a little more later until you completely wean yourself from sugar? You will have ditched the old habit and formed a new one without putting yourself under too much pressure.

If you have had problems saving 10% of your regular income (as recommended by experts) you might find it a lot easier to begin by saving 1%. Yes, I mean just 1% percentage until you are willing and ready to move to the next stage of saving. The spark and motivation you will get from that little victory will usher you further and earn you greater victories. Babies begin their walk by taking baby steps but baby steps never last forever, because as babies grow in stature and confidence, they take bigger, faster and steadier steps.

Have you been struggling to write a book for many years? Or would you have loved to write a book but find it impossible because you just do not know how to go about it? Begin the process by writing a few words a day, maybe 50, 100 or so, a day or even a week. Stick to the time and day you have set aside for writing, and you could soon end up with a beautiful book with your name boldly written on the cover. You do not even have to write a big volume for a start. Begin with just a mini-size one of about 5,000 words or so. That is all you need to stir your blood and become an accomplished author in the next few years. If you cannot write a book in 6 months, write it in one year or even in two years. Just do a little bit of it each day or every other day on a consistent basis.

The habit is more important than the victory, without the habit the victory will be outside your reach. If you always wanted to read a few books each year, but find it repeatedly difficult, it is likely you have been approaching things in the wrong way. Do not try to read twenty, thirty or more pages a day. Why not try to read just one or two pages a day for a start. If you keep to that, you will at least have completed reading a medium sized book in about three months. This should be an encouraging achievement for anyone who has never successfully read a book in a year. Many people never read a book in year, not because they have never attempted, but because they ignored the fact that most things we succeed at are the result of our habit. You can develop the habit of reading by taking things easy and steady.

Some Christians have never completed reading the entire Bible in their lives. Judging by my experience as a Christian, I believe the Heart cry of many Christians is to experience the fulfilment, benefits and sense of achievement that comes from reading the Bible from cover to cover. Notwithstanding, the joy of fully reading the Bible is only a dream for millions of God's children. The reason is simple. Many Christians want to imitate others who read through the Bible in six or twelve months. You do not have to impress anyone with the reading of the Bible.

I reckon that reading about five or more chapters of the Bible daily will probably help you finish the entire Bible in a year. If you find that overwhelming, you can find or devise a programme that is easier for you. You can read about two and a half chapters daily and complete the reading of your Bible in two years. It is entirely up to you if you chose to do this in 3 years or more. The dream of reading through the entire Bible is achievable if you take little by little.

Maybe you have been struggling to de-clutter your house or garage for many years, but have been unable to create the time, or you lack the motivation to do it. Therefore, if your intention is to do it over two weekends, why not start with the easiest items and carry out the de-cluttering over two weeks or two months. Start by just one small step each weekend. If you continue to wait until you can do it in a big way, it may never happen. To do the impossible, you will have to start from the possible otherwise things will remain as they are for a long time. Start from where you are, simply doing what you can.

The principle of developing mini habits, taking little strides and winning tiny battles is easily applicable to anything we do. Whether you are writing a university essay, increasing business customer base, making new friends, training for a marathon, preparing for a driving test, building up your vocabulary, breaking a bad habit or forming new ones, the approach is the same. I must emphasise once again that this is not about living with a small mentality. It is about dreaming big, but acting in small, manageable (often negligible) and effective ways until your dream comes true.

Feed Your Positive Habit, Bit by Bit

Feeding your habits gradually is a sure way of reinforcing every behaviour. Bad habits reinforced will lead to painful and regrettable endings. When strengthened, positive habits will build up to the point that a person's future will be greatly enhanced. Bad habits are difficult to break; good habits are more likely to be quickly abandoned. If you keep feeding a positive habit that is connected to your dream you will soon discover that nothing in the world can stop you from reaching your goal. Popular blogger and author, James Clear, suggests it is more rewarding to focus on forming habits, establishing and developing systems, than to chase after goals.

If you are a business person your goal may be to gain a 10% market share, while your system may be the sales and promotional activities that lead to this.
If you are a writer, your goal may be to write a 300-page book, while your system may be the number of pages and the schedule of your work to accomplish that goal.

If you are a tennis player, your goal may be to win the Wimbledon finals, but your system may be your daily training routine that will get you there.

If you are a PhD student, your goal may be to bag your doctorate degree, but your system will be the daily action plan leading to the achievement of your degree.

If you are a pastor, your goal may be to raise a 1,000 strong congregation; your system may be the daily evangelistic, assimilation, and equipping events leading up to that number.

Mr Clear proposes that although you may have a goal in mind, you should have an effective system (routines, activities and daily habits) which will serve as stepping stones towards your goal. When you master certain skills and weave them into your life habitually, you will stand a better chance of achieving your goals than people who simply have a dream and strategy, but lack the consistency to see it through.

Concentrating on targets could give you the impression that until you are there you are not good enough. Your happiness could be tied to when you successfully achieve your aim. It will be more beneficial for you to put your efforts into establishing and working a system (forming habits) that will enable you to accomplish your dream with relative ease. It is more profitable to create a habit around whatever you want to achieve. Goals are not permanent but habits can be permanent and powerful. Go for tiny and consistent steps. Keep doing what you are doing and things will build up until they reach a tipping point.

Create a New Identity

Creating a new identity and following the rules of simplicity is the easiest path to achieving greatness. According to James Clear, your identity is who you are. For example, someone can say, "I am an engineer", or "I am a teacher". Identity could also be related to nationality. For example, one could say, "I am British", or "I am an American." Your identity is based on factors that distinguish you from others and they could be internal or external traits.

People who focus on first building a new identity will find it easier to build enduring habits because by creating a new self (the new person they would like to become), they have created a mirror image of the type of person they believe they are. It is only at this point that they can start to believe new things about themselves. They will then find it easier to have a change of behaviour. If you are already behaving successfully in a certain way that reflect your goal, then it is easy for you to keep it up. If your behaviour works contrary to your goal it will never be possible to accomplish your mission. Your identity (the type of person that you believe you are) will spur you to develop corresponding habits that are fundamental to reaching your goals. Changing your identity or belief is therefore key to changing your actions. Simply because you have a dream does not mean your dream will come true.

It is your minuscule daily habits that will lead you to the future you yearn for. So decide the type of person you want to be and then, prove it to yourself with small wins, small steps and activities that glide you smoothly towards fulfilling your dreams. These little steps are very critical to shaping your destiny and bringing you, health, happiness and prosperity.

If your goal is to lose weight
Identity: Become the type of person who moves every day.
Little Steps: Purchase a pedometer: Walk 50 steps on the first day. Next day double that. The third day add another 50 steps (making 150). Do this 5 day a week- adding 50 steps each day and you will soon be amazed by your achievement.

If your goal is to become a published author
Identity: Become the type of person who writes 500 – 1000 words a day.
Little Steps: Write 50 words on your starting date. Keep this up each day a week. Developing the habit of a writer is more important than initially chasing after your goal from the start. Once you have developed the habit of a writer, you will soon be writing 1000 words a day and sometimes more.

If you want to be a prayer warrior
Identity: Become the type of person who intercedes every day.
Little Steps: Pray 5 minutes every day. Praying 5 minutes consistently on a daily basis is more important than trying (and failing) to pray 2 hours daily only to lose motivation along the line. Once the habit is developed, unconsciously (with little effort) you will come to a point when you begin to pray for long hours effortlessly.
Many people make New Year resolutions at the beginning of every year, setting targets for

themselves and never working on those targets beyond the first week of the year. The reason for this failure is not far to seek. They aimed high, may be too high (which is not so much the problem), but had not developed the daily habit needed to push things through. So, year on year they keep making resolutions and setting goals without ever coming close to their aim. Eventually, they give up and never try again. Smaller wins help to build and sustain motivation, engineer progress and strengthen your willpower. Form and develop little habits. Keep working on them in the direction of your goal. Stretch yourself a little further the moment you become comfortable with your daily routine. Big goals can be achieved through steady daily and persistent little actions. Just as tiny positive habits can make a person's dream come true, so also can little negative habits wreck a person's life.

CHAPTER FIVE

LITTLE FOXES CAN RUIN A VINEYARD

The Bible says, *"Take us the foxes, the little foxes that spoil the vines: for our vines have tender grapes"* (Song of Solomon 2:15).

The fox is a skilful, clever and subtle animal belonging to the dog family. A fox is tricky, sly and clever; it is sneaky, destructive and evasive. At the time this passage was written, vineyards were meticulously watched to prevent foxes from invading and destroying the fruits. Walls were used to protect vineyards from foxes and other pestilent animals from eating the grapes. Little foxes that spoil the vine is symbolic of little things that people do that defile and devalue them. In just the same way that little positive steps will generate outstanding outcomes, so also do little mistakes, little sins and seemingly harmless attitudes create stumbling blocks to an individual's progress and a Christian's relationship with God.

Many people would never tell a blatant lie or flagrantly break the law. Yet in some very subtle, unrecognisable ways, they may come short in these same areas. Telling half-truth, taking office property without permission, gossips, little bits of un-forgiveness and bitterness, occasionally or passively watching sinful programmes on TV, all make up the little foxes that can bring down a child of God. They may seem harmless- yet they are capable of making a lasting impact on an individual's life.

The little foxes in a person's life may not actually be sins, but could simply be some weakness or an area of vulnerability. It could be those little habits repeatedly carried out until they determine a person's destiny. It is very easy to underestimate their impact because their full force is never felt until it becomes too late. They can be found in every area of a person's life, and will vary from person to person. You must identify them and be determined to not let them derail God's plan for your life. Remember, they may be so insignificant that you need to work very hard to pin-point them. A mosquito may be very tiny, yet one bite from that insect can have such deadly consequences, that it can kill the strongest person on earth.

Little Choices Can Change Your Health

Health is one of the areas where many people do things that turn out to be not so good after a long time. Many of the killer diseases of modern times are the result or poor eating habits and lifestyles. The impact of poor eating may not be noticed in one, two or more instances. It generally takes months or even years for the impact of destructive eating habits to become noticed in people's lives. The results build up gradually, but each time you eat what you should not eat, something definitely happens. People often find it hard to give up bad eating habits even when they know there is only one end to it – bad health, and in many cases, untimely death.

Some people's unhealthy ways of eating may be due purely to a bad habit or for the sake of convenience. For some other people it is just because of the cravings they have for certain types of food at particular times, maybe when they are undergoing stress. Every child of God needs to remember that their body is the temple of the Holy Spirit, that God wants His children to enjoy good health. Being mindful of what you eat, particularly over a long period of time, is key to living healthier and longer. Daily little eating habits (good or bad) will determine the state of your health in the medium and long terms. God's Word says,

> *"What? Know ye not that your body is the temple of the Holy Ghost which is in you, which ye have of God, and ye are not your own? For ye are bought with a price: therefore, glorify God in your body, and in your spirit, which are God's"* (1Corinthians 6:19-20).

Step back and think before you grab that bag of fried potato crisps or a bar of chocolate. That extra amount of salt intake and the unnecessary quantity of sugar and sweet drinks consumed all add up, especially if it happens frequently. The quantities may seem negligible, but in the long run their combined effect can shorten a person's life. Cutting down on, or avoiding them altogether will not only benefit you physically, it will also bring glory to God because taking care of your physical health amounts to glorifying God with your physical body, the temple of the Holy spirit.

Not too many Christians will dishonour their bodies through adultery and fornication because they would not want to defile the temple of God or hurt the Holy Spirit. Unfortunately, a lot of God's children will care less about what they eat because they are not conscious (or pretend not to know) that wrong foods are just as dishonouring to their bodies as physical acts of sin committed with their bodies.

It is God's will for you to stay healthy, live longer and give Him more room and time to work through you. You are God's own vehicle designed to deliver His blessings to the world. The stronger and longer you live, the more you can do for God.

The little extras of bad food will combine over time to create an unhealthy individual. Whether the problem is with the quantity or quality, it will yield the same outcome if continued for a period of time.

Staying fit and healthy is of paramount importance to succeeding in life. You can keep your mind healthy by blocking off Satan's attack on your mind. Accommodating fear, anxiety and all forms of negative pre-occupations can overburden your mind and, together with other factors, can lead to poor mental health. Just like you nurture your physical body, you must watch what you allow into your mind. If allowed to persist, those thoughts can alter the entire course of your life. If you give them enough room and time, they will take firm root and could interfere with your mental health. Make conscious efforts to nip them in the bud and rid your mind of any demonic infiltration when they are still in the early stages.

Little Actions that Harm Relationships

No one can live in isolation. Life is made up of networks and team work. God never created us to be completely independent of others. Relationships are vital to your progress and success. It does not usually take a lot to build or destroy relationships.

Everyone must work at theirs. What you put in is what you get in return.

Your relationships with others can be used by God to uplift you beyond your expectations, but you must work at it to reap the benefits. It is true that not all relationships are productive; some actually do more harm than good. Nevertheless, most of the breakthroughs and open doors you will enjoy will depend on how you manage relationships. You must find out those little foxes that are damaging to the relationship between you and your spouse, parents, children, relatives and relevant others. God's prescription for getting the most out of relationships can be found in Colossians 3:12-14:

> *"Put on therefore, as the elect of God, holy and beloved, bowels of mercies, kindness, humbleness of mind, meekness, longsuffering; forbearing one another, and forgiving one another, if any man have a quarrel against any: even as Christ forgave you, so also do ye. And above all these things put on charity, which is the bond of perfectness."*

Do not expect to harvest what you have not sown into a relationship. If you are not willing to forgive, do not expect forgiveness from others. Many people expect way more from others than they are willing to give. Many times, we also expect from people what they are unwilling or unable to give. To make a relationship work you will have to go that extra mile that it needs. If you keep grabbing from others in a relationship and you are not playing your part, there comes a point when the other person will run out of patience or whatever you are benefiting from them. You do not have to give the same or as much as others put in, but you must be seen to be honestly doing your best to build and sustain a relationship.

There are so many little things you can do to enliven your relationship with others. Learn to value the people in your life, appreciate the little benefits you get from them. It makes them feel great. Never take offences too far. Sometimes the other person may not even know how far you have taken things. They may not even be aware that you are that hurt. Learn to have a short memory for offences. Speak to the person and iron out issues quickly.

Everyone needs a certain amount of space. Learn to understand when the other person needs a break. It may be longer than you are comfortable with, but understanding they need it at the time will help your relationship a great deal. Never fail to show that you care. Simply saying 'thank you', 'how are you', 'I love you', 'I miss you', 'I have been thinking about you', may be just about it. It could mean a lot for the people in your life. Failure in these simple ways could significantly hurt your relationships, especially if issues are not resolved on time. I have found that just remembering someone's birthday and other important dates is very powerful in strengthening relationships. The absence of care, love, respect, value, forgiveness, humility, and being inconsiderate are just some of the little things that the devil can exploit to destroy the link between you and others. The issues may seem minor but they can cause incalculable damage to your relationships. You might know of someone who does not ask for too much but simply wants to be appreciated, validated and supported for a relationship to thrive. Sincerely think of those little things that you can do that will turn that relationship around today, and just act on them.

Little Barriers to Personal Development

Failure to continuously add value to your life will make you less relevant to changing times. God wants you to reach out for a bigger and better life. Whatever your pursuits the way to increase your value is to keep adding something new to your life on a continuous basis. There are many little things people do which are capable of diminishing their worth. There are also many things people fail to do which subsequently obstruct their progress. For example, regular planning may not seem important, but failing to plan is the cause of many failures people encounter. Whenever a person fails to plan for the day, week or month things can become chaotic and left at the mercy of other events. It may not seem a big issue putting off tackling that project at the right time, but before you realise it, procrastination can very easily complicate matters and make life more difficult later. Initially this attitude may appear harmless, but over time the damage caused will be obvious and things will become more difficult to deal with.

Imagine your life without those daily distractions of phone calls, emails, and social media, uninvited and unwanted guests- I mean those things and people that breach the boundaries you have erected for your personal effectiveness. They may look harmless and insignificant, but allowed to continue for a reasonable amount of time, they can drain you of the energy, motivation and concentration you need to focus on building your dream. You need time to read inspiring and helpful books that will change your life and enhance your effectiveness. You need more time to nurture your spiritual life- reading your Bible praying and carrying out other spiritual exercises that will build your spiritual stamina.

Taking a major step towards dealing with time wasters will afford you the time you need to add value to your life on a daily basis. You can read, listen to tapes, pray and do other things that will accelerate your success.

The television is one of the greatest enemies of personal development. A lot of people are so busy daily that the only spare time they have is after they have returned from work. Unfortunately, many people spend that time glued to the television box. Of course, it is necessary to watch some amount of television daily to keep you abreast of what is happening around you. Nevertheless, too much of it does not give you room to read a book or listen to that valuable audio tape that could take you to the next level. You can be trapped, made passive and infused with negative emotions by what you watch on television. There is always a price tag on personal development. A deliberate, consistent and progressive approach is needed to make it happen because,

The information you have is not what you want.
The information you want is not what you need.
The information you need is not what you obtain.
The information you can obtain costs more than you want to pay.
Source Unknown

Obtaining one, two or more university degrees does not always provide fresh information for current issues. A lot of people never read a book about five or more years after they had their last graduation. They become too engrossed in family, professional and personal commitments at the expense of obtaining information and knowledge that will set them apart from others. Learn something new every day. Learn something little every day. If you read 5 pages of a good book every day, in one month you would have read about 150 pages. That is about the size of an average book. Therefore in 12 months you would have read about 12 good books; this will take your knowledge and understanding to a much superior level than the previous years. It will make you better at what you do. It will take your confidence, communication and development to an all-time high; all for just twenty minutes a day.

Psychologist, Abraham Maslow (1943) argues that people get motivated in life by seeking change and fulfilment through personal growth. He contends that people derive motivation when certain needs are met. He arranged the needs into hierarchical order:

- **Biological and Physiological**- such as air, food, drink, shelter, warmth, sex and sleep.
- **Safety**- such as protection from elements, security, order, law, stability and freedom from fear.
- **Love and the need to belong**- such as friendship, intimacy and relationship.
- **Esteem**- such as prestige, independence, achievement, status and respect.

- **Self-Actualisation**- which include the realisation of personal potential, personal growth, self-fulfilment and peak experiences.

Maslow proposes that peoples' needs move from first (basic) level to the highest level- the phase of self-actualisation. Some people have argued (and I agree) that people can still thrive without having their needs met in Maslow's order. Actually, I suggest that pre-occupation with some of the lower order needs (as proposed by Maslow) can become the little obstacles to personal growth. Maslow suggests that we will never be fully satisfied until we become self-actualised. Self-actualisation means attaining to self-fulfilment, self-satisfaction and becoming the best you can. This is achievable through deliberate personal development programmes, made possible by protecting your tiny time frames and utilising them meaningfully to repackage yourself for the market place.

Make personal development a lifetime commitment and you will make yourself almost indispensable in the places that matter. In a busy and highly demanding world, this can be sometimes challenging. Nevertheless, Jesus says in John 15:1-2:

> *"I AM the true vine, and my Father is the husbandman. Every branch in me that beareth not fruit He taketh away: and every branch in me that beareth fruit, He purgeth it, that it may bring forth more fruit."*

Every minute counts. Make time to build your skills, increase your knowledge and sharpen your understanding. It does not require plenty of time. You need a little amount of time repeated until you achieve your objective.

"Counting time is not nearly as important as making time count. I have only just a minute, just sixty seconds in it; forced upon me- can't refuse it, didn't seek it, didn't choose it. I must suffer if I lose it, give

account if I abuse it. Just a tiny little minute, but eternity is in it." – Source Unknown

What if you did not have to pick every telephone call, watch a little bit more TV, read non-essential newspaper and magazine pages? What if you used only designated time to access YouTube, Facebook and read emails? What if that time spent on your 'favourite' movies was focused on reading your favourite professional or business books bit by bit? Things will definitely become different for you after many months and years. Little wonder the psalmist prayed to God: *"So teach us to number our days, that we may apply our hearts unto wisdom."* (Psalm 90:12).

Little Excuses Hold People Back

Excuses may appear harmless, but they are usually the enemy's tricks to keep people bound and stop them from entering into new dimensions of success. We all have them, and we all make them- some of us are better at it. Excuses commonly given for not performing can actually be overcome. Excuses are used by the enemy to exclude people from their God-ordained programmes. People who habitually give excuses will hardly rise above the challenges they face. If you seek excuses you will find them. It is not always money, opportunities, education or background that stops people. Excuses are the greatest obstacles to progress. A little bit of it here and there keeps many people shackled to the point they never come close to realising their full potential.

Common Excuses that People Give

Every excuse has a solution, and we must look for ways to make things happen rather than accept reasons why 'it cannot be done'. Let us examine some of the most common excuses briefly:

I haven't got the time.
This is probably the most frequent excuse many people give. Truth is, if it matters to you, you will find the time. We naturally find time for things that we value most in life. If that thing is important, there will be time for it. It will find its way to the top of the list.

I am afraid of failing.
Every one entertains fears. In fact, the fear of failure is perfectly normal as long as you do not let it stop you from fulfilling your dreams. The difference between being a failure and success, lies in being afraid, and yet going ahead to do the things you are afraid of. Nelson Mandela states, "I have learned that courage was not the absence of fear, but triumph over it. The brave man is not he who does not feel afraid, but he who conquers that fear."

I need more time to perfect the plans.
Practice, they say, makes perfect. It is no use waiting for everything to be in a perfect state before you take a plunge. Staying passive and forever

planning will not initiate success. There are times when you need to plan thoroughly, but many other times, 'more time to plan' is simply an excuse to shy away from confronting a situation.

I do not have enough funds.
Money does a lot of things, I agree. I discover very late in life that many things can be achieved without money. Even businesses can be started on a 'shoe string'. Look for an aspect of what you want to do that does not require so much money. Having started, you are more likely to achieve or finish than someone who never took off.

I am not sufficiently educated for this.
Education is very important, but it is no longer a valid reason for lack of success in today's world. There is so much information around- on the web, libraries and other sources, that you can literally self-educate on just about anything. Search for the information you need wherever it can be found, and you will find yourself making progress in life. You probably have enough information and education to at least begin doing something about that goal.

I cannot take the risk.
A Chinese proverb says that *"Pearls don't lie on the seashore. If you want one, you must dive for it."* We all face risks every day, but I believe the greatest risk of all is the risk of not doing something you must do. Ultimately you could end up with a life full of pain and regrets.

This will be too difficult.
Most cheap and easy-to-obtain things have very low value. If you want to be great, be willing to go the hard and difficult route. You really do not have to work too hard to succeed all the time, this book is about taking little daily steps towards your goal until you triumph. You need God to bless you with divine wisdom to enable you to work smart. Of course, hard work is the old-fashioned unbeatable route to success- nothing can ever take its place. You can gradually develop your work ethics if it is a challenge to you. Just take it little by little.

Too many people are doing it.
Too many people may be doing it, but the best is yet to come. That is why someone will always come around to do better than many who are already there. Even if you do not aim to be the best in your field, you can simply be your best. That might just be enough. Who knows what happens from there! You will never know unless you try. Start from somewhere today.

I know people who have failed at doing it.
You will also find a lot of people who have excelled at doing it. For every failure in a class there are usually tens of success stories. Why not trust in yourself (I should say, your God) that you could be one of the success stories. Step out with that mindset and expect God's help.

I am too young.
Many young people around the world have done wonders. You can be one of them. You are never too young to do exploits. Jeremiah was young, David was young and Joseph was young. They did things many older people (including their leaders) could not do. Be thankful to God that you are alive at a time when there is an explosion in knowledge, and technology is constantly transforming the way we do things. You are never too young. With God on your side all things are possible.

I am just too old
You are never too old to achieve great things. Nelson Mandela became president at the age of 76. Ronald Reagan became U.S president at the age of 69.

Colonel Harland Sanders started KFC at the age of 61. The Ancient of Days is backing you. Age has its own advantages, and you are welcome to maximise the benefits of age. Age cannot stand in the way of anyone who really wants to achieve a goal.

This is outside my comfort zone
Comfort zones are 'death' zones. Staying in the region of comfort is akin to staying in a boring, unadventurous and uninspiring realm. Get out of your comfort zone and strive towards those great things you have always wanted to achieve. Dare to do something new and you will break new grounds. Start small, go steadily and grow your confidence until you can 'fly'.

Excuses gradually wear away a person's will and motivation to accomplish great things. Find ways to overcome whatever is standing between you and your destiny. A person who refuses to give or accept excuses will be unstoppable in life. Choosing to give an excuse about something is often more dangerous than the actual problem people face.

The Man Who Wrote a Book with a Blink

Jean-Dominique Bauby demonstrated the power of little things when he achieved the unthinkable under impossible circumstances. Bauby was a French journalist who at the age of 43, and after an unfortunate accident, suffered a serious stroke. The incident left him paralysed, completely speechless and only able to blink his left eyelid. Although he lost the use of his mouth, arms and legs to the stroke, he did not let this deter him from doing the unusual. His condition notwithstanding, he went on to write a book that would later become a best seller titled *The Diving Bell and the Butterfly,* by simply blinking his left eyelid. He wrote a complete book by blinking when a system called Partner-Assisted Scanning repeatedly recited the French alphabets. Bauby dictated one letter at a time in ten months. The first 25,000 copies of the book were sold out in one day (Guardian online, 27 January, 2008).

Bauby could have simply given up hopes of living, instead he chose, not only to live, but to write a book in such a poor state of health. He wrote a best seller, not because of his extraordinary story, but also because the book was very well written. This was all the result of very little, inconsequential, almost hopeless steps. You too can do it. If Bauby blinked and wrote a book in ten months, you too can get your fingers on the keyboard or put your pen on paper and write at least a book in twelve months. You may not be interested in writing a book. That is fine. Whatever it is that you have been thinking of doing, just take little, gradual steps and you will be there sooner than you can imagine. No more excuses. If anyone has done it, yes you can. If no one has done it, you can try. Giving excuses erect barriers to progress. Do not let excuses stand in your way.

The Psalmist says *"For by thee I have run through a troop: by my God have I leaped over a wall"* (Psalm 18:29). Even when you are afraid, or have genuine reasons not to go ahead, why not bring your fears to God and continue to rely on His ability to see you through? If you are faced with a wall, God will be there at your invitation to lift you over it only if you will first try to climb over that wall. Just take that first step.

The Tongue: A Little Member that Sets Ablaze

The Bible says,

> *"Even so the tongue is a little member, and boasteth great things. Behold how great a matter a little fire kindleth!"* (James 3:5).

The tongue may be small, but it wields so much influence over the life of an individual. With the tongue people can inflict wounds on themselves and other people. The tongue can start off little troubles, little battles and even great wars. The tongue can also communicate blessings or curses. God's main purpose for blessing us with the tongue is for positive communication, encouragement, liberation, praising Him and for blessing others. With the tongue we can raise the dead, but anyone can also send people to the grave through the tongue. The Bible talks extensively about the power of the tongue.

The Tongue that Curses

The tongue was never designed by our maker for cursing, but unfortunately the Bible says, *"Therewith bless we God, even the Father; and therewith curse we men, which are made after the similitude of God"* (James 3:9).

Words spoken by God's children are living and powerful, because we have the Spirit of God in us. We can also speak powerful and life-giving words like God does. You owe yourself a duty to speak blessings and not curses into your life and the life of others. This is your responsibility. This is your calling.

The Tongue that Slanders

The American Heritage Dictionary defines slander as:

"The utterance of defamatory statements injurious to the reputation or well-being of a person... A malicious statement or report." Slander involves saying unsavoury things about people to the hearing of others. Examples are false witnessing and false accusations. Slander thrives where there is strife, contention and division. The Bible says those little slanders could destroy your neighbour, because death and life are in the power of the tongue. When you speak negatively about people, you sow seeds of discord in other people's hearts about your victim. This could lead to closed doors, lost opportunities, withdrawal of favour and soured relationships. The tongue may be little but if misused it can cause so much havoc.

Anyone who chooses to slander others will also reap the consequences. God hates slander and will judge everyone who destroys others with their tongue. Sometimes it is the little things in life that are more difficult to manage. Many people can manage major crisis but when it comes to the tongue, they have very little control.

The Lying Tongue

Lying takes a Christian back to the days before they got saved. It may not cause you to lose your salvation, but it does make you behave and look like an unsaved person. Hence the Bible says, *"Lie not one to another, seeing that ye have put of the old man with his deeds"* (Colossians 3:9). Lying downgrades your spiritual worth. It is hated and forbidden by God. Lies may seem little and show no immediate or obvious repercussions. They can, however, gradually erode the foundation of a person's spirituality. Not only can it make you feel guilty, it makes you unfit before God. Many Christians habitually live a lie. Lying can obstruct the move of God in a person's life. No matter how little it is, a lie is never in the interest of any child of God.

The Talkative Tongue

Some people get their tongue too busy to their own hurt because they have no control over it. *"In the multitude of words there wanteth not sin: but he that refraineth his lips is wise"* (Proverbs 10:19). It takes discipline to control the use of the tongue. Many strong people can be terribly weak when it comes to the use of the tongue.

If you talk too much you will hardly escape sinning. The fewer the words you speak the better for your spiritual health. It is by far safer to speak less than speak too much. Talking unnecessarily can easily let out secrets or paint a wrong picture of who you truly are. You will also be at the risk of speaking at the wrong time or saying the wrong things. What you can say with ten words do not say with twenty words.

The Self-Destructive Tongue

Many Christians need to be reminded over and again that life and death are in the power of the tongue. When you speak negatively about yourself or your condition, you are very likely to get what you say. Words are seeds; words are arrows; words are bullets and each time you speak negatively of yourself you are turning arrows and bullets against yourself. Only speak what you want, what you expect and what you will appreciate should it happen in your life. Each time you speak unwholesome words about yourself, you have sown bad seeds. If you cancel those words immediately, then you will have destroyed those seeds and prevented them from sprouting and taking root. But if you keep saying the same things persistently, you will be nursing and nurturing those negative confessions until they produce negative outcomes. God's Word says:

> *"Say unto them, As truly as I live, saith the LORD, as ye have spoken in mine ears, so will I do to you:"* (Numbers 14:28).

Do not invite trouble into your life by the things you say. Overtime it all adds up to determine the direction of your life. Life tends to go the way of your confession, positive or negative. An individual who keeps saying wrong and unscriptural things should not expect positive outcomes because we reap whatever we sow.

CHAPTER SIX

THE POWER OF THE FIRST STEP

Whatever you plan to do, the first step is always the most important. It may be little, slow or wobbly. It may even be scary and uncertain; yet, unless you take that first step you are going nowhere. No matter how frightened you are about taking it, the moment you do, you will be on your journey to success. You will be better placed than many people who are still at the level of intention and desire. If you take the first step God will see you through the rest of the process because, *"The steps of a good man are ordered by the LORD: and he delighteth in his way"* (Psalm 37:23).

God cannot begin to order your steps unless you have started to move in the right direction- the direction of your dreams and visions, the direction of your calling and mission. Jeremiah was very much aware that God has the power to bless and direct the steps we take: *"O LORD, I know that the way of man is not in himself: it is not in man that walketh to direct his steps"* (Jeremiah 10:23). If you keep hesitating to make the initial move towards your goal, you will be trusting in your own ability and wisdom. Begin by faith because God says, *"When thou passeth through the waters, I will be with thee; and through the rivers, they shall not overflow thee; when thou walkest through fire, thou shall not be burned; neither shall the flame kindle upon thee"* (Isaiah 43:2). Even if you have fallen several times, God still has a strong word of encouragement for you. He says in Isaiah 43:19: *"Behold, I will do a new thing; now it shall spring forth; shall ye not know it? I will even make a way in the wilderness, and rivers in the desert."*

If you do not move, God cannot move on your behalf. He instructed Moses and the children of Israel to go forward when they were stranded by the Red Sea, awaiting the worst from their Egyptian enemies. *"And the LORD said unto Moses, wherefore criest thou unto me? Speak unto the children of Israel that they go forward:"* (Exodus 14:15). The children of Israel went forward, and the Lord proved Himself mighty by destroying the Egyptians, but until they took steps forward it was not possible for God to divide the Red Sea and make a way for His people. God will always make a way, but He expects you to first act in faith before He provides what you need to cross over to the other side. When you set aside your fears and other inhibitions, the Lord will show up in your situation.

One Step at a Time

I find the following quotes thought-provoking and helpful:

"To get through the hardest journey we need take only one step at a time, but we must keep on stepping" – Chinese Proverb.

"You don't have to see the whole staircase, just take the first step." – Martin Luther King Jr.

Everyone needs some kind of change from time to time. The thought and journey of change can sometimes be scary, especially if it is a major change. It can be so frightening and confusing that it may be difficult to know exactly where to begin. To help you deal with your apprehension and hesitancy, you may find the following questions helpful:

1. **Do I have a dream?**

   I bet you do have a dream because every person on earth has one, or should have one. Even if you have a beautiful dream, lack of action will turn it into a daydream. Everyone's dream is different. Some dreams are humble while others are noble. Your dream may never win you a Nobel Prize. It is your duty to make it a delight to spring into action without delaying it till tomorrow. Your dream may have originated from childhood or your adult years, the important thing is that you have a dream. The size is immaterial, what is more important is the fulfilment you derive from your dream. If you have a dream, go for it without any more delays.

2. Do you believe in your dream?

If you do not believe in your dream, no one else will. The name you give your dream is what people will call it. The way you take it is the way people will relate with it. Believe in and protect your dream from dream 'killers'. They are all over the place and may be close friends and relatives. They may also be total strangers who will give you every reason why they think your dream is unachievable. Protect your dream like you would protect an unborn or a newly born child from untimely death. You must give it life by making the initial move.

3. Are you prepared to leave your comfort zone?

> The place where you feel at ease, undisturbed, secure and not having to face too much inconvenience is your comfort zone. The place beyond which you are not usually

prepared to go, although you know you must, is your comfort zone. You know that going beyond that point will take some challenges, inconvenience and cost. The comfort zone is a danger zone. 90% of people prefer to remain there, just because total 'death' in the zone does not occur immediately. It happens slowly and unnoticed until the situation cannot be remedied. It is the sphere of mere survival, fear, complacency, unhappiness and averageness. People who chose to remain here prefer to hold back because they are too afraid of what the next step holds for them.

Many people wait until something disastrous, compelling and outside their control forces them out of this region. Life outside the comfort zone is exciting, adventurous, and often leads to financial freedom. Real life is lived outside the comfort zone. True comfort resides outside the comfort zone. People who live there have no regrets. They break barriers without getting 'broken'. People who live outside the comfort zone do something they have never have done before so they can get the results they have never had. If you cherish your comfort zone you will never take the first step towards building an enviable future.

4. Are you prepared to make mistakes?

People who do not make mistakes are probably

making nothing new. If you attempt something new, you will likely make mistakes the first time. The fear of making mistakes is the mother of all failures. People who are not afraid of mistakes are always trying and learning something new. They are always finding and benefiting from something new. They are constantly changing their own lives and the lives of other people. Take the initial step and experience something new today.

God does not teach us everything in one day. He does not expect us to learn everything all at once. He takes things step by step even though He has great plans for us: *"Whom shall he teach knowledge? And whom shall he make to understand doctrine? Them that are weaned from the milk, and drawn from the breasts. For precept must be upon precept, precept upon precept; line upon line, line upon line; here a little, and there a little"* (Isaiah 28:9-10). The important thing is to avoid making the same mistakes repeatedly.

Taking the first step in accomplishing your dream is the only way you can achieve your goal, and if you miscalculate you will learn from your flaws and take the lessons with you for life. The fear of errors is actually the biggest mistake anyone can make. Failure aids growth, lead to experience and helps you to learn new things. Take the first step, be prepared to stumble, learn and make up for any setbacks.

5. Are you prepared to forget your past?

People who fail to break free from their past may find it difficult to enjoy the present. They cannot step into the future. If you do not let go of past failures, hurts and disappointments, there will not be much hope for the future. A lot of people are so bogged down by their past experiences that they hesitate to look or move ahead. The Bible says,

"Wherefore seeing we also are compassed about with so great a cloud of witnesses, let us lay aside every weight, and the sin which doth so easily beset us, and let us run with patience the race that is set before us, looking unto Jesus the author and finisher of our faith; who for the joy that was set before Him endured the cross, despising the shame, and is set at the right hand of the throne of God" (Hebrews 12:1-2).

Do not let your past define you, and never let anyone define you by your past. God is the God of new beginnings. You will not be able to change your past, but you can change how you allow the past to impact on you. Put the past behind you and take a step forward. Keep things moving one step at a time.

6. Are you ready to take the first step?

The only way to be ready is to start before you are ready. You will never be fully ready because you are not perfect. The first step will not get you to your destination, but you will never get to your destination without it. It involves taking chances, but unless you take chances, you stand no chance of success. In physics we were told "an object at rest tends to stay at rest" unless a disruptive force sets it in motion.

Many people die with all their talents, knowledge, wisdom and skills. They die in fact with all their potential because they never had the courage to step out into the dark. On the contrary, many people who are less talented, but more courageous have gone on to accomplish great feats because they dared that demon called fear and beat it hands down. Anyone who cannot conquer his fears is unlikely to conquer other 'enemies' of progress.

7. Are you ready to pursue your dream steadily until you win?

The beginning of anything is the preamble to its completion. You must keep going until the game is over. It is critical to have a dream. It is imperative that you believe in and pursue your dream. Mistakes are part of the game, if you are not making them you are probably not learning, and when you make them you must encourage yourself and put them behind you. Try not to bite too much at a time, the lighter the better. The next thing you must learn is the courage and discipline to keep going, keep winning (or failing) until you emerge victorious. Never let go; stay consistent, persistent and ruthless about achieving your goal. Eliminate distractions, overcome discouragements, learn your lessons and grow into the person you have always wanted to be.

Action Creates Traction

Dreams only come true when they are pushed through. Every driver on the road today once had a nerve-wracking experience the first time they sat behind the wheel. Many things in life are simply like that, every worthwhile venture will have the fear factor before the wow factor. No high jumper begins their profession from the top. The same applies to the boxer, pilot, diver or mountaineer. The initial attempt could be the scariest of all. Notwithstanding, every expert in any field, had to grapple with those moments of doubts before they became celebrated in their fields. If you continue to worry about what will happen if you failed, you will never discover what could happen if you tried. Never be afraid to dream big, but never be in a hurry to take on too much. It is better to take things easy than to give up quickly.

Motion leads to momentum. Over preparation can lead to procrastination. Many dreams remain unrealised under the guise of preparation, unreadiness and the need for more time. Until you spring into action, you will never be in motion and will never gain momentum. Nobody or circumstance can confine you within any walls except the walls you build for yourself. Break down those barriers, bring down those walls, pull down those obstacles and become free to express yourself. There are too many people who constantly think about:

Writing a book but never did.
Learning a new skill but never started.
Starting a business but are waiting forever for the right time.
Starting some charity work or social enterprise but are waiting endlessly for an opportune moment.
Starting a movement but never made the first move.
Doing a PhD programme but too scared to take off, even though they know they can.

Losing weight but cannot be bothered to take the first step.
Stopping a bad habit that would save their life and save them money, but are waiting for some day before they begin.

Although some people have failed several times, they still believe that they can do something remarkable with their lives- a few go ahead to start all over again, but others simply gave up and preferred to wallow in self-pity and excuses. Life is a journey. Success is also a journey. Begin the journey by doing something about your dream today.

Bold and Courageous

When you go ahead to attempt the things you are afraid to do, this is courage. When you first started to walk, you needed courage to take the very first step. It was probably the most courageous thing you ever had to do. Yes, you had many falls, bruises, pains and even probably gave up for some time. Then you grew up (with encouragement from parents and others) you kept on walking until you could run, skip, jump and dance- all by yourself. You were brave and desperate enough to keep trying. Whatever your dream now, you need that same dimension of bravery to start and finish.

The Lord once told Joshua:

> *"Have not I commanded thee? Be strong and of a good courage; be not afraid, neither be thou dismayed: for the LORD thy God is with thee withersoever thou goest"* (Joshua 1:9).

Are you thinking of stepping out into a new and uncharted territory? Are you thinking of doing something notable for yourself, your family or for God? You need courage to damn the consequences, call the bluff and take the plunge. What is the worst-case scenario? Failure, embarrassment, discouragement, rejection, loss, ridicule and probably much more. You have no way of knowing whether these potential negative outcomes will materialise. Most failures are the result of the fear of failure which stops people from leaving their comfort zones.

If you are too afraid to come out of your hiding, you will never experience the light of success. Without courage you will never realise your dream. It takes courage to go the extra mile. It takes courage to step into the unknown, to say no to unhealthy habits and relationships. It takes audacity to stand up and be counted, or to keep away from those foods that you definitely know are harmful to your health. Jesus asked Peter to step out of the boat, and walk on the waters.

If you lack courage even after God has spoken to you many times about doing something that will bring you remarkable success, you will still ignore God's voice. You will keep looking for better ways to start. Peter did step out. His faith wavered and he began to sink but the Lord was right on hand to keep him above the water. Daniel was threatened with being thrown into the lion's den. Daniel knew the threat was real. He knew it would cost his life if he was thrown into the lion's den as a punishment for disobeying the idolatrous authorities. Yet he refused to be moved by their threat but did what was right and God moved to rescue him from death by shutting up the mouths of the lions. Fear will never go away but opportunities come and go. You cannot break new grounds, expand your horizon or experience new victories without having the grit to do so. Theodore Roosevelt once said:

"Far better it is to dare mighty things, to win glorious triumphs, even though checkered by failure, then to rank with those poor spirits who neither enjoy much nor suffer much, because they live in the grey twilight that knows neither victory nor defeat." If you fail after you have tried, it will be on record that you dared to do something, but if you fail because you failed to try, it will be on record that you never tried at all. So, dare to dream, dare to do; take the first step today.

Newton's Three Laws

The great British physicist and mathematician, Isaac Newton, developed three physical laws that explain the relationship between a body and the forces that act upon it. The laws also describe the response of the body to acting forces. These laws are referred to as Newton's laws of motion. The first states every object in a state of uniform motion tends to remain in that state of motion unless an external force is applied to it. The second states when a force acts on a mass, acceleration is produced, and a greater mass will require a corresponding amount of force. And, the third law of motion states that for every force, there is a reaction force of equal size, but opposite in direction. We will look briefly at only the first law and relate it to the need to make the first move towards our goal as quickly as possible.

Newton's First Law of Motion

Called the "Law of Inertia", Newton's first law states an object that is at rest will stay at rest unless an external force acts upon it. An object in motion will remain in motion without changing its speed and direction unless it is acted upon by an external force. This suggests that naturally people will keep doing what they are doing (resisting change) until an external force intervenes. People are naturally inclined to keep doing certain things in the absence of a strong external influence.

There is always a tendency to become too relaxed until we become rattled by some external force, such as loss of job, sickness (maybe due to bad eating habits), failure in business or academics or some other dramatic event. It would be more beneficial to take the first step today to deal with a problem or situation that could end in regret, reproach or shame. It is more rewarding to take the first step towards achieving that dream than to wait until your competitors, negative circumstances and some painful and regrettable occurrence forces it on you.

The Four Lepers: "Why do we sit here until we die?"

In the days of Prophet Elisha, the city of Samaria was surrounded by Syrian forces, who besieged the city until the Samaritans ran out of food. It was such a hopeless situation. God's people were boxed in and there was no escape route. In this state of hopelessness, there were four lepers suffering a similar fate with everyone else. However, they had a different attitude towards the situation. They had a few options, and only one of them would eventually get them out of trouble and imminent death:

Die of starvation within the city.
Remain at the entrance of the city and die.
Get into their enemies' camp, probably resulting to death.
2 Kings 7:3-4 tells the story of these four lepers:

> *"And there were four leprous men at the entering in of the gate: and they said one to another, why sit we here until we die? If we say, we will enter into the city, then the famine is in the city, and we shall die there: and if we sit still here, we will die also. Now therefore come, and let us fall unto the host of the Syrians: if they save us alive, we shall live; and if they kill us, we shall die."*

The lepers had a dream and desire to be saved from famine and delivered from death. It was a difficult and hopeless period not only in their lives but in the lives of all the inhabitants of the city. They had a choice to stay where they were and die slowly and painfully of hunger, but they chose to take the first step towards the solution rather than fearing, cowering and hoping something would happen someday. Though gripped with fear, the lepers rose up suddenly and went towards the camp of the Syrians who had laid siege to the city. When the lepers arrived at the camp, the Syrians were nowhere to be found. What happened?

> *"... the Lord had made the host of the Syrians to hear a noise of chariots, and a noise of horses, even the noise of a great host: and they said one to another, Lo the King of Israel hath hired against us the kings of the Hittites, and the Kings of the Egyptians, to come upon us"* (2Kings 7:6).

As the lepers moved, God chased their enemies out of the land. The Syrians fled their camp leaving behind their tents, horses, asses, including money and other items as they fled. This marked a turning point in the lives of the lepers who made a move without knowing what their plight would be, without knowing what would befall them. God never disappoints when we demonstrate acts of faith in line with His Word If you do not take the first step, how will you ever tell what could have been? Keep taking those little steps- the unstable, frightening baby moves that can open up a world of unbelievable possibilities. These were people who stood no chance within the community, people who were disregarded, isolated and unwanted. They became news bearers, problem solvers and history makers because they acted in faith, and God honoured their faith.

The food and everything else left behind by the Syrians were enough to bring about a major change in the life of everyone who lived in the city. God may well be preparing you to be a change agent where you have been ignored and isolated. This will not materialise unless you turn your vision into action in the smallest way you can start with. Acting opens you up to God's intervention. Taking further and continuous action (they may seem meaningless) will continue to open you up to constant help from God. When you decide to confront the enemy, your problem, or move in the direction of your dream, God will go with and strengthen you all the way.

CHAPTER SEVEN

THE POWER OF COMPOUNDED ACTIONS

Life is meant to be a process- in many respects, a process that involves accumulated little actions. These actions build up to make or break anyone, to construct or destroy a person's future. In today's world everyone wants to succeed overnight and with minimum effort. We want the crops to produce and be harvested in 24 hours. We want the microwave to work faster than it presently works. We want a 10-hour flight to be cut to 2 hours if possible. People want their academic qualifications to take shorter durations. We fall in love with anyone that tells us 'it can be done very quickly', even if they are deceiving us. People get hoodwinked, cheated and ripped off very easily because everyone seems to be in hurry and wants things to happen now. There are many people waiting to prey on us because they know we are in an age when people want everything to happen right now.

If you keep eating high-calorie food beyond the recommended amount on a daily basis, it will not be long before the body reflects what it has been fed over time. Your overall health will soon reveal signs that you have been eating unhealthy food over the months and years. There will always come a time that the habit we have developed over time will translate into obvious results. The results may be negative or positive, resulting in a life of poverty or prosperity, happiness or frustration.

The Concept of Kaizen

Kaizen is a popular quality management concept which originated from Japan, and has spread to many parts of the world. It is characterised by continuous little improvements to processes, services and products. The concept can be applied to every aspect of our lives. Translated into English, this Japanese word means 'continuous improvement'. The principle which was developed and used in the 1950s and 1960s is still applied today by many Japanese companies. It has also spread to many western organisations across the world. Some of the key elements of Kaizen include:

Elimination of waste- of time, money, materials, resources and efforts. Incremental improvement to systems, processes and daily activities. Discovery of the underlying cause of mistakes. A focus on process or systems improvement rather than being result focused.

Kaizen is more or less a habit or lifestyle, a continuous process of making minor but continuous adjustments which could result finally in impressive and gigantic accomplishments. It is a picture of evolution rather than revolution, consistency instead of immediacy, step change instead of quantum leap. The Bible says, *"But the path of the just is as the shining light, that shineth more and more unto the perfect day."* (Proverbs 4:18).

We can completely overhaul our life by finding those little, regular and result-oriented ways to make continuous progress.

All things are Possible

If you can sit back and determine negligible ways to accomplish major things within a period of time, there is nothing that can stop you. Maybe you want to:

- Earn a PhD
- Read the Bible from cover to cover yearly
- Fly first class around the world
- Start and grow your own business
- Become an international best-selling author

- Stay alive till you are one hundred years old by staying fit and healthy
- Buy and live in a mansion
- Become a movie star

- Run a marathon
- Become financially independent
- Be the best husband or wife in town
- Become a university professor
- Climb the highest mountain in the world
- Go on a yearly cruise or your dream holiday
- Win an Olympic gold medal
- Speak two or more foreign languages
- Learn to play a musical instrument

Whatever the dream is- it may look crazy, noble or humble, if you can develop the daily habits it takes to move towards them, if you can be incremental and consistent at doing those things, nothing will stop you. Stop worrying about the size of the problem; start changing your attitude; little by little and with fortitude the dream will become real.

Sadly, too many people either do not believe that basic steps can lead to major changes or they simply lack the patience and perseverance to stick to tiny routines for a long time. Some people have concluded it is too late to go down the route of the old fashioned, step by step, and slow and steady way of pursuing success because they have missed opportunities in their early years. You can always start from somewhere or start something else. God did not create you to have only one life-time dream. You are never too old to dream again.

The Bible says even the old people shall dream dreams. You can always use age to your advantage because you will have learned what the younger generation take for granted. You will have discovered that every minute really counts, and be able to maximise the use of your time. So, go after your goal and let God help you to do whatever it will take to achieve it step by step. All things are possible for those who put their trust in God, and for those who can get rid of old and unproductive habits and form new healthy ones.

If you want to develop new habits, John Maxwell suggests you create three columns. Write all of your current habits that support your current dream in the first column. In the second, make note of your current habits that hinder your progress. In the third, note down the new habits that you hope to cultivate as you move toward your dream. Then work hard to eliminate your unhelpful habits as you create or consolidate new ones that will help you fulfil your goals and objectives.

My Positive Habits	My Negative Habits	My Desired and Productive Habits

The habit change process

Choose to Sow Positive Habits

Most seeds are usually very tiny, but the yield that results from them can be phenomenal. Habits are exactly like seeds. What you sow you reap. If it is positive you will have a positive harvest, and if it is negative the outcome will be negative. Thorns will produce thorns; poisonous plants will produce after their own kind. Consistent thoughts of failure, evil and defeat will produce corresponding results. If you sow the positive, you will reap positive results. People who sow oranges reap the same. Those who sow apples definitely reap apples. It is unusual to sow good seeds and reap the opposite.

The quantity you reap is usually significantly more than what you sow. A seed of maize will normally produce cobs of maize. An orange seed will produce several oranges which in turn contain several seeds. If you do not sow seeds, you will reap no fruits. Seeds sown are never harvested immediately. It takes time to reap what you sow and what an individual reaps today is the product of seeds sown in the past. The quantity you sow will determine your harvest. Similarly, the quality you sow will determine the quality of your harvest. If you sow healthy seeds, you will get a healthy harvest, all things being equal. If what you sow is weak, unhealthy and unviable, you will reap correspondingly in the long run. Anyone can become great, any person can achieve outstanding success by breaking their dream into daily achievable steps.

Doing little things is not enough to take us very far in life; we could actually get stuck at the bottom. The aim of this book is to highlight the power of little things, minuscule activities that can translate into massive achievements. A lot of people simply need the courage to take the first small step, and continue to increase their strides until they grow in confidence and capacity to achieve great things.

Abandon Old and Build New Habits

We are the total sum of the habits we have developed over the years. Harmful habits are formed one step at a time in the same way that helpful habits are formed. Good habits can be liberating and help you to gravitate towards greatness just as unhealthy habits can be harmful and lead to a downward spiral. Take for example, snacking. Whereas it is great to snack on healthy foods such as fruits, nuts and vegetables, a lot of people prefer to go for the unhealthy ones such as potato crisps and high-fat products. These can lead to unhealthy weight gain, heart diseases, diabetes and other health problems. The question is why are people not giving up their 'killer' habits? It is because bad habits will never go away without a fight. This does not suggest that habits are impossible to change. If a person is determined nothing can stand in their way. If a person spends two hours watching TV or movies daily, that is an equivalent of:

14 hours weekly

56 hours monthly

672 hours yearly or

28 days yearly

Even if you reduce the number of hours spent watching TV to one hour daily, that still stands at:

7 hours weekly

28 hours monthly

336 hours yearly or

14 days yearly

These figures are frightening; just by watching TV habitually (for whatever reason) for one or two hours daily, a person is spending either 14 or 28 days of their lives yearly before an electronic box, gazing at information and pictures most of which are useless and add nothing positive to their lives. However, if on the reverse, a person forms the habit of reading just about five pages of a book daily, probably taking about half an hour to do so, this positive habit will mean that the person would be reading a medium sized book of about 140 pages every month. By the end of the year the individual will have read about twelve average sized books. We can change or replace any habit the moment we have decided that we have had enough.

Three Critical Elements of Habit Change

According to Dr Fogg, the Director of the Persuasive Technology Laboratory in Stanford University, three things are critical to successfully forming new habits. They are:

- **Level of Motivation.** You must have a certain level of motivation regarding the habit you want to develop, if not you are not likely to succeed.
- **Ability.** You should at least be able to do what you want to do. It is no use trying to form a habit in an area where you lack the ability.
- **Trigger.** The trigger you need is the thing that reminds you to take the actions that will make your habit stick. Whatever you want to achieve- floss your teeth, do push ups, lose weight- it does not matter. You still need a trigger. It could be that before taking a shower every morning you must do some press-ups. Your trigger is the shower. As you continue to link your daily press-ups with your daily shower, you will soon find that the exercise has become a habit to you.

Below are other examples of linking a new habit with something you already do. Something you already do can form the foundation for the new habit you would like to develop.

After I _____, I will
_____

After I _____, I will
_____

After I _____, I will
_____

For example, this could be: *After I brush my teeth, I will floss my teeth (two top and two bottom).*

After I turn off the lights to go to bed, I will thank God for something.

After I get off my bed in the morning, I will pray for 5 minutes before leaving my room.

These are simple suggestions. You can design your own plan with whatever is important to you. If you link your new action to an existing behaviour, things will become easy. Then, you will need no special reminder, extra motivation or stringent plans to make it happen.

Aggregation of Marginal Gains

As you develop the minuscule daily habits that align with your life goals, be it climbing the highest mountain in the world, losing weight and keeping fit, saving money, writing a book or any project, it may look like an exercise in futility in the beginning. But as you keep going slow and steady without looking back, the little actions will turn into mighty achievements. The danger is in not initiating the process. The second problem is in trying to focus too much on the goal rather than on the process. Success is a process. You will need to hold on tightly to the process (the daily, weekly and monthly targets), remain consistent until you achieve success.

Jeff Olson in his book, *The Slight Edge*, illustrates the working of the slight edge (daily little actions) on a person's life using the two sides of a pair of balance scales. When you go through difficult and critical times in life, it can be assumed that the scales have tipped badly down towards the negative side. This could be because in some important aspects of your life you may have made some bad choices for many years. But then, you can turn things around in those same areas by adding just a little bit of good, corrective positive habit on the positive side of the scale- one little action at a time without stopping. Something will be happening to gradually balance the scales or tip it heavily towards the positive side (resulting in progress, financial freedom, happiness, weight loss, etc.) without being noticed. If you continue to nurture the positive side, the negative side of the scale will continue to lift gradually until there is a balance, and then the scale tips completely downwards to the side of success.

So, it is never too late to succeed, it is never too late to change an old habit or build a new one. It is not too late to start something new in your life today; if you have never dreamed of doing greater things, you can start today. If you have lost hope of dreaming, you can find somewhere to begin in a small way today, continue to build until you succeed at reversing the negative and downward trend you may already be experiencing.

A pair of balance scale

It may take longer than you expect but if you refuse to give up you will reap the benefits of your efforts. Never be afraid to think big or act big, but break your goals down into small achievable parts. It has to be every day and not once in a while. If you chase after greatness too suddenly it might eventually elude you; but if you start from the ordinary and work gradually towards the extra ordinary, you will end up with greatness. Long term consistency is more rewarding than short term intensity. Never underestimate the power of tiny daily activities.

Keep the Momentum

Momentum is a terminology used in physics. It is defined by Merriam Webster dictionary as *"the property that a moving object has due to its mass and its motion"*.

It also means: the strength or force that something has when it is moving or the strength or force that allows something to continue to grow stronger or faster as time passes. Momentum is the force accumulated by a series of events. A moving object has a certain amount of momentum, but an object standing still has no momentum. If you make the first move, momentum takes off. If you keep it up, momentum keeps growing and there will come a point when the speed you have accumulated makes additional action literally effortless, because the momentum is on your side. As you take little effortless steps in your success journey, momentum building becomes really important. But to do this you will have to overcome the force that stops you from beginning in the first case.

Momentum is the fuel for motivation. The thing you always wanted to do will remain an idle dream unless you begin doing. It does not matter how insignificant the first step may look. It may be just the first phone call, filling out a form, simply registering an organisation, searching the web for the information needed, sending an email or taking a trip to see what others are already doing. Once you make the initial move, follow it up quickly with successive (little) daily actions towards achieving your dream. Momentum will set in and continue to grow, making things easier with every added activity in the direction of your goal. The little things we do require momentum to make them result in laudable accomplishments.

Never Lose Momentum.

Just as momentum can be gained, so can it be easily lost. It is advisable that when you start to build a habit, never miss twice. If you missed your action once, do everything you can, never to miss it the second time as this can make it difficult for you to continue. If you begin to lose momentum you will start to experience some difficulty becoming steady with your progress. Remember Newton's First Law of Motion? A body in motion tends to remain in motion while a body at rest tends to remain at rest. This means that once you start and gather pace, it becomes much easier to keep going. Success will beget more success, victory will lead to more victory.

Similarly, if failure and negative habits are allowed to gather momentum, they will continue to thrive and eventually result in undesirable consequences.I have a personal habit of praying about many issues in the long term. Generally, I strive to pray about these matters on a daily basis and have not stopped for several years. I have found that those prayer items are much easier for me to pray about no matter how tired I feel. The act of praying simply becomes effortless, refreshing and fulfilling each time I take on those prayer items. A few people who are close to me sometimes wonder why I limit my daily prayer to a few- just between three and five at the most.

The power of momentum means that a strong dimension of God's power and presence is often demonstrated in those areas of my life and ministry because of cumulative effective praying. Whatever you do- praying, writing, business, weight gain or loss, learning a new skill or language, if you keep doing things modestly and consistently, momentum would soon set in. You will be certain you are making progress, and because the routine gets easier with time, you will be able to stretch yourself from the current to the next level without giving up on what you are doing.

Speed and size are important but they are less important than momentum and progression. As critical as goal-setting is to your success, taking realistic, achievable daily steps is what will get you there. Momentum requires patience and persistence because it does not happen in one day. Momentum gives you peace, speed and ease. You know momentum has set in when a small additional step on a daily basis makes it feel or look like you have put in so much into your project.

Set aside specific times daily and weekly when you should do something about your project on a consistent basis. It has to be every day for you to reap the gain. When you set big objectives, break it to the smallest levels possible, work on it daily, let it gather and build speed, keep doing what you are doing without giving up.

Inspiration does not last forever, motivation can be short lived, but momentum is what will bring in those beautiful moments that you long for. Loss of momentum can be likened to a large ship that has been on full speed for several miles. When the captain suddenly pulls back the throttle to the 'stop' level, the ship keeps going. It does not stop suddenly, and therefore no one realises quickly that something is happening- that the ship is slowing down gradually to a stop. It keeps going because it is still living on the momentum it had already gained. That is the power of momentum.

It is crucial to never take your foot off the throttle, never pull back from the accelerator, never apply the brakes when things start moving in your favour. Always bear in mind how long it has taken you to get to where you are, and that it is only in so far as you keep applying constant pressure that you will achieve your goal. If you are taking daily steps to overcome an old and difficult-to-break habit, avoid a break or slow down. And, if you are building a new habit, keep doing what you are doing until you accomplish your goal.

Avoid Momentum Killers

You should at all cost avoid momentum killers because momentum, if gained, will not last forever unless it is constantly fuelled by the same activities that preceded it. Keep finding ways to improve on what you do. Remember that when something becomes a routine, as will be the case for those who really want to succeed, people tend to fall into the trap of boredom and rut. At such times all you need do is to keep doing the same thing but in more creative and exciting ways.

Another momentum killer is inability to manage success. Some people become arrogant, incorrigible and too relaxed when they begin to experience success. Never let go of the little things that paved way for your success, instead find ways to make things better. Whatever helped you to get there, stay with it and improve on it, bearing in mind that, in most cases what got you to a certain level of success is unlikely to keep you there permanently.

CHAPTER EIGHT

KEEP MAKING PROGRESS

Dream big, think big but keep the process simple until you have gained enough confidence to take on bigger actions. Whatever you set your eyes upon, it is the same principle. It is about habits, little habits formed, developed and retained within a period of time. When you read and hear of the great things people have achieved, you can easily become intimidated, but you must never be impacted negatively by other people's success. You do not have the same calling, mission or aspirations. Their definition of success may be different from yours, their values may be far removed from yours. Appreciate your individuality and uniqueness, and trust in God's ability to help you. It is not about anyone else, it is about you. When you start make sure you get to the finishing point.

Pursue Your Purpose

Some people desperately want to succeed materially. They want cars, money, houses and such like. They want to go on holidays and travel around the world. A good number of people will do anything to accomplish these, but this may not be you. Yours might simply be to succeed emotionally, be happy, enjoy good and flourishing relationships, overcome low self-esteem and be at peace within you. Another person may want to be an academic or simply have a good education. This is equally worthwhile, and may be all they want in life. You are the only one who knows what you want from life. Failure occurs for different reasons. The best response to failure is to dust up yourself and keep going. When next you get to a difficult bend, apply the knowledge gained from the last encounter with failure and move on.

Some people who suddenly become rich by winning the lottery also end up abruptly in poverty, because they have never learned the humble and steady way of building up wealth, one layer at a time. On the other hand, the majority of people who amassed their wealth gradually and steadily, following time tested principles and processes are more likely to retain their wealth, sometimes for generations to come. It is possible to take a walk in a dimly lit street for as long as you want. In the same way, when you have something in mind to accomplish, do not worry about all the details at the beginning. Do not be frightened by the challenges you face or the uncertainties ahead. Do something now, and never stop doing a bit every day. Knowing where you are going and making progress towards it is more relevant than having your destination in full view.

Find the Miracle in Your Obstacle

There is a miracle concealed within every obstacle. Obstacles will show up in different sizes and shapes. They will also require varying efforts and resources to overcome. There is always a way round or out of every barrier you may face as you set out to accomplish anything. Always remember *"... that all things work together for good to them that love God, to them who are the called according to His purpose"* (Romans 8:28).

It is impossible to walk and never stumble once in a while, but the good news is that the number of times we stumble is often less than the times we remain steady. Every day will have its own share of challenges even when you are taking on less challenging projects. Climbers walk to mountain tops one step at a time. Even though the journey is filled with many obstacles, they will find a way round until they reach the mountain peak. Some will fail to finish their climb and return to it at a later date. Others will persist because they have put in several years of preparation.

The Chinese Bamboo Tree

The story of the Chinese bamboo tree is an awesome lesson in patience and perseverance, keeping a routine and staying with your dream for as long as it takes. You plant the seed like you would any other seed and expect it to sprout and grow. But then, you water and fertilise it for one full year with no noticeable results, no sprouts no growth. Then you continue the process of watering and fertilising the following year with no sign of life springing up. Then comes the third year- and as usual you continue to water and fertilise it- the seed fails to respond to your efforts. No sign of life, not even a bump on the soil surface to indicate something is happening. The fourth year comes and it is the same story.

Then in the fifth year, as you continue to water and fertilise the seed, something suddenly happens! The bamboo tree not only sprouts, but it shoots out, grows up and reaches a height of ninety feet in six weeks!

The question is, did the bamboo tree actually blossom to an astonishing height of ninety feet in six weeks? The answer is an emphatic no! All the years you have been watering the seed, something positive has been happening. Nobody knew it, not even the farmer, let alone observers. All the efforts of the previous years had been paying off without notice.

Many things we embark on do not yield results instantly or quickly, and when you look at other people whose lives appear to be flourishing, you may become troubled and discouraged. The best attitude to life is to keep doing those little things that will lead you to breakthrough. Learn to embrace obstacles because, in every obstacle there is a hidden miracle. Find the miracle in your obstacle. Give God the chance to turn things around for you.

There is a Lion in the Way

Proverbs tells us that a lazy person claims there is a lion in the way- the way of progress, success and victory. *"The slothful man saith, there is a lion in the way; a lion is in the streets."* (Proverbs 26:13) In other words, many people fail to take even the first step because of the obstacles in the way. In reality, there may be a lion in the way, there may be all sorts of genuine reasons why one may not step out into achieving their dreams.

No matter how true the obstacle may be, God will always make a way if you hand the situation over to Him. Paul wrote, *"... a great door and effectual is opened unto me, and there are many adversaries"* (1Corinthians 16:9). Every worthwhile dream will have an adversary, an obstacle, something to contend with. Paul wrote a large proportion of the New Testament. He had God's call. He had a dream but there was much adversity in the way. He did not give up God's call just because he faced challenges. He knew that as long as he was steadfast, with God's help nothing would be able to stop him. The same Paul later wrote in 2 Timothy 4:7-8:

> *"I have fought a good fight, I have finished my course, I have kept the faith: Henceforth there is laid up for me a crown*

of righteousness, which the Lord, the righteous judge, shall give me at that day: and not to me only, but unto all them also that love His appearing."

Sometimes after taking that very important step you may still encounter a brick wall, but then you must find ways to overcome your limitations. You will never know how close to the blessings you are, how easy things would have turned out until you act. Until you arise you cannot shine, and you cannot experience the glory of the Lord.

How Long Will It Take?

When you begin to take steady, easy steps in the direction of your dream, the issue is not how soon you get there (at least, not initially) but it is whether you get there, and whether you finish well. I read of a man who desperately wanted to be a renowned author. He had put all his efforts and resources into writing what he thought would be a powerful and bestselling book. He had hoped that after publishing that book he would go on to become known, and probably end up a prolific author. After finishing the manuscript of his first book, he approached a publisher, and he was rejected. He went to another, hoping all should be well at this time, but he was wrong as he was once again rejected. This man did not give up. He kept trying.

His best efforts at seeking a publisher for his book simply ended up with more rejections until he got to a total of 30 rejections. This time around he could take no more. Discouraged and devastated, he wrote himself off and abandoned his dream of ever becoming an accomplished author. He picked up his manuscript and dumped it in the trash to at least, help him to avoid the torture he would endure from repeatedly seeing the document. Fortunately for him, his wife retrieved the manuscript from the bin and encouraged him to have one more go at resubmitting it to a publisher. That was it! Not only was the book accepted and published this time, it later went on to become one of the bestselling books ever. Sometimes we give up just when we are only a step away from victory. Many people have found themselves there.

The story of this man is one of perseverance, endurance and discouragement. We all undergo similar experiences in our journey to success. For some the struggle is pretty much the same as the one I have just narrated. Some people have had it less agonising, while others have had things much more challenging. One of the lessons to take away from this account is that whatever happens, whatever you do, never give up just because things are not working out the way you want. Stick with your dream and stick with God- He will ultimately make a way.

CHAPTER NINE

THE POWER OF LITTLE IDEAS

Ideas are thoughts that generate in our minds intentionally or unintentionally. Ideas can be borne when brain-storming, but they can also spark off when we are completely at rest, busy and at very odd times. Ideas can be so little and faint that many people will give them little consideration. Everything ever created is a product of someone's idea- airplanes, ships, skyscrapers and spacecraft. Just look around you and you will find that everything you can see is the outcome of ideas. Yet many people had similar or better ideas, but never acted on them. We all have ideas, and no idea is completely useless. Many people have had their ideas rejected by others, and the same ideas eventually turned out to be celebrated across the globe. Never ignore or let anyone kill your ideas.

An idea can be your personal thought, an intention, your perception or view. It is not how many ideas you receive that matters, it is the quality, source and what you do with them that is important. Ideas are like tangible raw materials you need to create what you need in life. Nothing can be created or recreated without an idea. You may not be able to reach out and touch an idea, but you can feel it from within you when an idea touches you. You will know that something has happened to you. An idea can have a slight effect on you, but sometimes it can have such a gripping impact on you.

Ideas are Like a New Born Baby

Ideas are like a tender new-born baby. When they are born they are fragile and tiny, and parents would need plenty of patience and hard work to get them to grow into maturity. Babies need to be delicately and painstakingly nurtured in order to survive and thrive, and so do ideas. If a child is not protected and provided for, he may not survive. The same thing can happen to an idea that was never cherished, protected or developed. Within every one of us are thousands of ideas which when harvested can completely change our lives and those of people around us. Ideas are common to everyone. What makes the difference is what we do with them as they come to us.

Ideas are Fragile and Fleeting

Ideas are not only fragile, they can easily fly away. They can disappear just as quickly as they appear, unless they are swiftly captured. The key to preserving your ideas is to waste no time before writing them down. It is better to scribble down your ideas on any form of paper, with the bluntest pencil than to let them escape. Everything in existence became a reality because someone dared to do something about their ideas.

Stop your ideas from flying away by recording them as quickly as you can. They will come to you as you sit on your sofa, at the lounge, during a flight, as you visit a bookstore, online and in the bathroom. Ideas can visit in the kitchen, at the dinning or in the gym; where ever it is, every idea is for a reason and a season. Capture your ideas, work on them and bless the world with that special gift that God has given you.

Why you should Capture Your Ideas

An idea that is not written down may fly away forever. Ideas are probably the greatest tool you have to become successful in life. When you write them down, you are able to focus automatically on the issues. It moves from the realm of mere ideas to the initial process of becoming a reality. Putting that thought down on paper helps you to focus on it and begin the process of making it real.

Another reason to promptly capture your tiny ideas is that memories fade very quickly. Your most valuable and beloved idea can quickly be lost unless it is written down. We frequently have gleams or beams of light flashed into our minds for a short moment, and then, very swiftly they can disappear from our minds. Because ideas do not stay with us for long, the faintest ink is always better than the strongest memory. Note-taking permanently traps down your ideas until you are ready to turn them into something tangible.

Writing down your thoughts also has the advantage of helping you to avoid brain overload. Whatever you deliberately write down you can easily let go from your mind, instead of working hard to remember it together with other things you have banked in your mind. Putting pen to paper helps you to de-clutter your mind and create room for more information.

Writing down your ideas can aid your ability to organise your thoughts. At first you may find that you have written things down in a messy order. But then you can come back and reorganise things into various categories or topics and put them in an orderly manner, in a way the information can become more useful to you. Things generally become clearer later when you write them down. When ideas first come to mind, they may feel very great, however, when you write them, you will probably find that the mind did not quite get things right. This discovery may be because as you write, you tend to clarify or analyse the initial idea; in some cases, you may find that the idea is more powerful or less powerful than you initially thought.

Organise Your Ideas

It is a great idea to note down your ideas. However, ideas like everything else, need to be organised for them to become usable. After developing the habit of writing down your ideas you will find that you now have a sea of ideas or information. Unless you organise these in an orderly manner, you will soon find that your efforts may not be worth it, after all. You will need to group your thoughts into similar subjects and in their order of importance.

When you start to organise your ideas, you will most certainly find that some ideas are simply dumb, and were probably not worth noting down. At this point you will be able to separate the chaff from the wheat. The great ideas will be differentiated from the not-so-great ones. It is perfectly alright to initially record everything that comes to mind and afterwards do a clean-up by eliminating the ones that you do not wish to focus on. The next thing to do with your written ideas is to devise a plan of action. What would you like to do with the information you have written? When would or must you act on them? What steps are you ready to take to make them a reality? What help do you need and where can you find this help? In what practical ways (in the short, medium and long term) can you turn your ideas into reality? Ideas that are not acted upon are not worth having. Ideas that are not acted on can lead to regrets, and can negatively impact on your destiny and the destiny of others. Ideas are instruments of progress, and only a few things in life are as powerful as great ideas. Flesh out your ideas, fight for them and fly with them. The LORD said to the prophet Habakkuk:

> *"...Write the vision, and make it plain upon tablets, that he may run that readeth it. For the vision is yet for an appointed time, but at the end it shall speak, and not lie: though it tarry, wait for it; because it will surely come, it will not tarry" (Habakkuk 2:2-3).*

Writing down the idea is the first step in the process of fleshing it out, the first step of giving life to your God-inspired thoughts. Ideas must first be expressed in words before they can effectively be translated into things.

Good Idea versus God Idea

No human ideas can match up with the ones planted in your mind by God. God's idea can visit you as you read your Bible. It can also jump at you when you are praying (this happens very frequently to God's children). God-inspired ideas can flash up when you are listening to someone preach the Word of God. It may come in the form of dreams, inspiration and revelations. Sometimes they may appear vague and unclear. Most powerful ideas never come in powerful ways.

Good ideas are thoughts that originate from our natural mind- they can equally be great and many of them have resulted in massive breakthroughs across the world. The greatest enemy of any idea is fear, inaction and failure to see it through.

How We Receive Divine Ideas

The Bible says:

> "For thou wilt light my candle: the LORD my God will enlighten my darkness". (Psalm 18:28)

> "In that day shall the deaf hear the words of the book, and the eyes of the blind shall see out of obscurity, and out of darkness". (Isaiah 29:18)

While you do not always have to wait to hear from God before you do everything, it is important to remember that God knows everything. He sees the end from the beginning; He knows and understands everything. God sees the whole story of everything. He does not expect us to abandon the common sense He has given us, but human nature is imperfect, and many times people find that had they sought God's opinion, about ideas that even appeared bright and promising, they would have saved themselves a lot of heart-aches. There are several ways you can decide whether an idea is from God or it is simply a personal perception (which in many cases, can be great).

God's Word is the number one way to determine whether an idea is from Him or from somewhere else. This is made clear in the Book of Psalms: *"The entrance of thy words giveth light; it giveth understanding unto the simple"* (Psalm 119:130).

God's Word is the light bulb that lightens the mind of His people. Meditating on His Word makes us think like Him, and connects us to the divine source of inspiration and revelation.

Praying, fasting, worship, and meditation are generally times that God breathes His spirit of ideas upon His people. When you are actively engaged in spiritual activities that connect your spirit with the spirit of God, it is common to get fired up in your mind or your inside. It is usual to find things welling up within you which you can confidently say originate from God. These experiences are normal ways God helps us to know what He wants us to do. Failure in Christian life is partly due to the fact that when God inspires us, we either fail to completely step out in faith or we are too afraid to go all the way with the instruction He has given us. Another dilemma is that we have too many ideas we do not know what to do with them. They all need to be organised or grouped in such a way that it will be easy to implement them.

An idea from God can sometimes be a test of your faith. Frequently, God's idea will stretch a person's faith to the point that he or she will have to pray and depend on God for the grace to step out with it. God's idea can sometimes be overwhelming and frightening. You may find that it drives you back to God to ask for His help. God's ideas are better than the best any natural mind can generate.

CONCLUSION

This book has highlighted the importance of mastering the details in whatever you do. Anyone who cannot conquer the little things of life may never achieve greater ones. A lot of people get a boost from the challenge and rewards of taking a giant leap, yet such people may be overpowered by the discipline required to accomplish lesser things.

Most large organisations have no problems planning ahead. They have no difficulty setting goals or crafting long term strategies to enable them fulfil their business objectives, but this is not always true for individuals. Inability to find easy ways to inch towards the achievement of dreams is a common reason why many people fail.

The emphasis of this book is not about small dreams and visions. Neither has it to do with mediocrity and living an uninspiring and unchallenging life. It is about finding tiny ways to travel that long journey. It centres on developing the discipline and endurance that will help you to advance towards your dream. It is about mastering the little things that will open the door to great accomplishments.

When a large establishment sets out a major goal, their overall objectives however lofty they may be, are shared out in time and space in such a way that various departments are only concerned with little parts of the process. Each part may count for nothing on its own even though it is an essential component of the final result. It is the interplay between an organisation's departmental contributions that forms the bedrock for their success.

It is not always the big things that make a relationship succeed. It is the little things which are often taken for granted. Things like 'I am sorry', 'I was wrong', 'thank you', 'I love you'. Tiny acts of kindness may be all that your partner needs to help maintain trust and keep the relationship running smoothly. It is the little gestures and acts of favour at work, in your neighbourhood and your social groups that may cause you to stand out as a person of influence amongst others. It may also be the little things that you failed to do to others- the tiny acts of kindness, or a simple smile at a neighbour- that will define their relationship with you. A little lie, broken promises and failure to keep appointments may all appear harmless, over time their outcome could be more powerful than anyone will imagine.

Negative habits that have been formed over the years can be adjusted or replaced by gradually undoing the past, one step at a time. It may take long, but not initiating the process can lead to a painful end. If it is a problem with eating too much, a person can gradually reclaim their lives by taking minor steps to reduce the quantity of food consumed; the person will progressively develop healthy eating habits once again and avoid the negative consequences of unhealthy eating. The same is true for people who want to altogether avoid certain types of food that could harm their health- one day at a time, one step at a time and one month at a time. You can significantly reduce the fear and stress associated with doing anything by taking bite size, doable and cumulative steps on a continuous basis.

Never Ignore the Little Things

Do not under-estimate the power of little things. If you consistently take care of them you can end up with great achievements in your life. Learn to start from where you are, use what you have and keep working hard at your goal.

The extra sugar and regular bar of chocolate, the extra one or two hours of sleep, and unnecessary time spent watching TV programmes are not harmless- they can hamper a person's progress. Many great people fall because of seemingly harmless things, even after they have successfully overcome major obstacles in life. People hardly stumble over big rocks, it is the little rocks, and the banana peels that trip people over, so take care of the little things at all times.

Never be Afraid of the Giants

All things are possible to those who believe. Never be afraid of the giants that confront you. Running away from problems will not get them solved, but having a plan in place to tackle them gradually is a sensible way out. All the people called and commissioned by Jesus could be regarded as 'weak'. Many of them would probably have been written off by modern society, but the Bible says:

> *"For ye see your calling, brethren, how that not many wise men after the flesh, not many mighty, not many noble, are called: But God hath chosen the foolish things of the world to confound the wise; and God hath chosen the weak things of the world to confound the things which are mighty; And the base things of the world, and things which are despised, hath God chosen, yea, and things which are not, to bring to nought things that are: That no flesh should glory in his presence"* (*1Corinthians 1:26-29*).

I believe Jesus deliberately chose people who had personal and other limitations. Yet these people went on to do colossal things for God. All you need to do in addition to your personal effort is to draw grace from God to succeed in whatever your dreams are.

People around you may become weary, others may tell you that you can't, but the Bible says those who wait upon the Lord will renew their strength; they will mount up with wings as the eagle's, they will run, and not be tired; they shall walk and not faint. Trust God for that great vision you have, take a 'bite' of it on a daily basis and ask God for His divine enablement to press on until you hit your target.

What is that in Your Hand?

Stop worrying about what you do not have and what you cannot do. Focus on what you can do, no matter how little it may seem. Every initial step you take towards a goal is a seed. When you sow and nurture that seed, you will soon discover the power of a seed. God could have created the entire world in one day, but He chose not to. He planned for it to happen in 7 days. The human race started as a seed in the form of Adam and Eve. Today we have billions of people all over the world. As you take steps to use the little you have in the form of energy, talents, knowledge, and whatever it is, God's grace will enable you to do what you could only dream of in the past.

Samson only had the jaw bone of an ass, and with that he killed a thousand Philistines. Why? Because he dared to approach the Philistines with the only thing he had, the little he could do, coupled with the power of God. Moses had a simple rod in his hand. God wanted him to do great things. God will use us to do anything so long as we are willing for Him to work through us. Moses was not sure of himself, neither was he sure of his rod, but once he stepped out by faith armed with just a rod, God took over the rest. The children of Israel approached the walls of Jericho without guns, and artilleries. God simply asked them to blow some sound with rams' horns. He asked them to march around the city for 7 days and then the miracle happened. The walls of Jericho came down flat.

In the days of Elijah, God shut up the heavens in response to Elijah's prayers, so it did not rain for the space of three and a half years. Then it was time for the land to have rain again. Elijah prayed several times for rain. Eventually there appeared in the sky, a cloud the size of a man's hand. It was a little cloud, but it resulted in a downpour. God will bless your little efforts if you will trust Him to take control. Rather than giving up, give it all to Jesus. Believe in God's faithfulness and ability. Believe also in yourself, in the great work God has done in your life these past years.

Keep taking those tiny steps towards your goal; eliminate every crippling habit one step at a time. Adolf Hitler once suggested that the easiest way to take charge of a people and have total control over them is to remove their freedom a little bit at a time, and do this by a thousand tiny almost unnoticed bits. This way, the people will not be aware that their rights and freedoms are disappearing until it becomes too late for them to do something about it.

Hitler was an evil genius, so he devised simple, easy ways to get people trapped and ensured they turned out the way he wanted. He took people by deceit, and by entangling them one step at a time. In a positive way, you and I can turn great problems around through tiny but steady steps. You can conquer that mountain one bit at a time. You can fulfil that dream one day at a time. If you have already taken the first step, have the courage to take the next. There is nothing wrong in growing slowing, but there is a big problem with standing still. Falling frequently is better than failing to walk, because no matter how many times you fall you will still be better than a person who refused to walk. In life, the only action that is guaranteed to fail is the failure to act.

Little Things That Matter

BIBLIOGRAPHY

Aggregation of Marginal Gains- Harvard Business Review: How 1% Performance Improvements Led to Olympic Gold
hbr.com

Habits, Not Goals
Jamesclear.com

Thandiwe Chama: Youth of Action
acelebrationofwomen.org

Jean-Dominique Bauby: Guardian online, 27 January 2008

www.ingramcontent.com/pod-product-compliance
Lightning Source LLC
Chambersburg PA
CBHW071122090426
42736CB00012B/1985